MW01193685

MODERN ALCHEMY

How to Transform a Lethargic
Organization Into a High-Performing,
Winning Machine That Is Greater
than the Sum of Its Parts

AYMEN ALMOAYED

Ballast Books, LLC
www.ballastbooks.com

ISBN: 978-1-964934-78-5

Printed in the United States of America

Published by Ballast Books
www.ballastbooks.com

For more information, bulk orders, appearances, or speaking requests,
please email: info@ballastbooks.com

MODERN ALCHEMY

History is littered with stories of legends, stories of seemingly superhuman individuals who join a lethargic team, an organization, a state, and immediately trigger a change of trajectory, leading to one small win after another, building momentum and ultimately allowing the group to reach incredible heights.

Every culture records stories of these legends in its oral history—stories of magicians and magical demi-gods that can turn copper into gold, a losing team into an international franchise, a desert into a global destination. We are not referring to those who work quietly alone in a dark cabin, opting to be a recluse from society regardless of output; we are referring to those with enough grit not to be a recluse and with enough systematic thinking to instead mold and bend the environment around them to create social machines that produce greatness.

Simply put, this book is a celebration of those special ones. It is the start of a movement to recognize their sacrifices and show gratitude for their discipline and for the value they have created.

In celebrating them, we remember the saying that imitation, even in its most primitive manner, is the best form of flattery, and therefore, we dissect their actions, analyze their algorithms, and copy their movements, always aspiring to create value as they do.

A glance or two at these examples quickly confirms that there is an underlying shared algorithm or theme, a set of principles that are honored by these special ones, these magicians, these Alchemists. This book initiates the process of shedding light on this reality.

Modern Alchemy, although seemingly magical, is completely logical and truly intuitive for those who have the wisdom to stop and meditate on the principles set out. The same way that yeast looks magical when a few grains are able to raise the large loaf of bread' Alchemy too looks the same from outside.

We refer to it as Modern Alchemy because while the old celebrated the magic and mystery, we celebrate the logic, the cerebral investment, the sacrifices, the discipline, and the mastery that make it all look so simple and so divine.

This book celebrates how one individual can nurture the hopes and aspirations of the members even of a country or a continent, can embed faith in a painful process to allow members the mental ability to continue, and can with one word or one phrase activate a voluntary marching army to change the world.

For those who celebrate and appreciate mastery, for those who humbly aspire to it, for those who wake up in the morning thinking of the ripple and impact that they'll leave behind, hoping that it lasts as long as possible, this book serves as a simple tool, the beginning of a conversation, and the start of an incredible journey.

Dedicated to my wife and my kids, Yousif and Isa, for being the reason.

To my uncle and role model, a noble giant who passed on too early but whose impact ripples to this day.

To a friend and a wise and regal Alchemist, His Highness Sh. Nasser bin Hamad Al Khalifa, Personal Representative to His Majesty the King of Bahrain and the Kingdom's National Security Advisor—may he always have the "golden touch." We have worked together on so many change projects that I can no longer tell where His Highness's thoughts end and where mine begin. His Highness is therefore in every page—if not in name, then in spirit.

TABLE OF CONTENTS

CHAPTER 1

THE HYPOTHESIS

C lose your eyes and imagine. Imagine someone who can take cheap lead and seemingly effortlessly turn it into valuable gold.

Imagine the demand for such a person. Imagine the possibilities. Imagine if you could recruit that person. Imagine if you could be that person.

This is what I call, in my lexicon, an Alchemist.

Alchemist

(noun)

- a person who practices alchemy
- a person who **transforms or creates something through a seemingly magical process**

We've all heard legends of men and women who had seemingly magical, sometimes divine-like abilities to create wealth and value and alter the course of history. They were sought after by kings, queens, presidents, chief executives, and even investors for their ability and because they changed outcomes and circumstances with their skill and their knowledge.

Simply put, they tipped the scale in favor of the sovereigns, patrons, teams, communities, partners, and clients they serve. These types always were and always will be in high demand wherever they opt to go.

Now imagine if their ability were neither divine nor mere superstition. Imagine if the ability to turn "**lead into gold**" and **create value where there was none—or only some**—were **neither supernatural nor magic**. Imagine if it were real. If it were learned. If it were acquired.

This is the hypothesis, the theory, behind this book.

From my observations and experience, I would argue that the skill of turning something dull and invaluable into something shiny and highly sought-after is one that is gained and refined with practice. It takes time and demands **purposeful and methodical focus**. It's like a muscle that you build with specific tools and specific habits and routines.

But what is important is that it can be learnt. It can be taught, and it can be scaled.

Now, let's extrapolate this premise and superimpose this metaphor even further. Imagine, instead of changing single, individual pieces of metal into gold with the limited upside of that application, if you could convert organizations or team into "gold-making machines," into high-performing, highly scalable, and highly efficient innovative and ever-evolving "organisms." Instead of one "goose that lays golden eggs," imagine creating an ever-multiplying flock of geese.

That is Modern Alchemy.

It is the learned skill of converting an existing failed, lethargic, or subpar group or organization into that "ever-multiplying flock of geese."

It's infinitely more valuable than simple one-off alchemy. And what's more, this, too, can be learned, taught, and scaled.

What Modern Alchemy Is and Who It Is For

I fully appreciate that the alchemy metaphor might conjure images of secret formulas and perfectly timed luck that results in *eureka!* moments and instantaneous magical benefits and results for an organization or career. To be clear, Modern Alchemy does not do that; it is not a magical potion, nor is it a special pill.

Modern Alchemy addresses a need to change a group or organization from its current state to a better future state. It clearly presents principles, observations, and tools, explained and laid bare before you to test, measure, and confirm to your satisfaction. These are key concepts and tools that can help identify or refine skills needed to make the necessary change.

The magic of Modern Alchemy is collecting, streamlining, simplifying, and linking these concepts and tools together, producing aspirational outcomes for those who diligently apply these learnings.

Simply put, Modern Alchemy is about **change** and **change management**. It is about aspirations and the hope for a better state. It's about introducing the tools needed to make that change and the commitment needed to overcome challenges and barriers to reach that destined state.

Modern Alchemy is the journey of moving from your "**current state**," an unwanted state of affairs, and heading closer to your "**intended future state**," a more preferred state of affairs.

There is a lot that has been written about successful organizational change management, about project management, about strategic planning, and about implementation plans. A lot of what was written is very well suited for large, already well-established organizations with worldwide recognition that have deep pockets; a niche; a seemingly monopolistic advantage; great maneuverability; access to immense resources; and the ability to offer a global talent pool best-in-class compensation or future prospects, let alone the amazing perks.

Let's be realistic. The reality is that the lives and challenges of one of those stellar already seemingly best-in-class entities—the likes of Facebook, Amazon, Apple, Netflix, or Google in the tech sector; the likes of Versailles, the Louvre, or the Tate in the museum sector; the likes of Harvard, Cambridge, Oxford, or MIT in the education sector; the likes of 10 Downing Street and the White House in the government sector; the likes of the Bill & Melinda Gates Foundation in the philanthropy sector—are very different from the lives of generic small and medium enterprises or organizations. I would go as far as assuming that the techniques and tools that apply to one may not at all be valid or applicable to the other.

A lot has been written about and for those great ones, yet not enough has been written for the rest who are striving for greatness.

For those stellar ones—for the incumbents—talent and partners, capital and authority already flow to them with minimal effort. For everyone else, I would suggest that the current paradigm in leadership, management, and strategy thought and advice the world over seems to be lacking. It sometimes "puts the cart before the horse," assuming abilities that, in reality, are strictly within the realm of incumbents only.

For example, "Just get the best talent," they say. It is simple: "Recruit the world's top talent. Find a niche. Be disruptive. And focus on culture, not strategy. Simple. Do this and your winnings will follow; the rest will solve itself."

This comical advice might be beneficial to a few incumbents, those household names, the ones with continuous solicitation from the world's top talent, minds, and capital. "Like attracts like," they say. But what relevance does that have for the rest of the world?

"Hire the best talent in the world" and "Remember to have a financial war chest" isn't advice at all. It's pseudo-advice, meant to sound good but not to get results.

For a new mega-startup or an incumbent with limitless resources, indifferent to immediate financial returns and geographic limitations, and with access to the best talent pools in the world, this recipe might be beneficial. For everyone else, the value of such advice is limited if not nonexistent.

So what if you're currently not the Facebook, Amazon, Apple, Netflix, or Google (FAANG) equivalent of your industry or region? What if you're a small, privately held software company in the Rust Belt of the United States? What if you're a third-tier university in rural England? What if you're a firm in a small country most people in the world couldn't place on a map?

What do you do when you discover that the "top talent" that every author, consultant, and TED speaker talks about is unavailable in your region or at your price point? Simpler yet, what do you do if your partners and investors are not the sophisticated, informed, and connected institutional investors recommended by the texts? What do you do when your boards of directors do not consist of internationally renowned and informed personalities? What do you do if the organization's legacy employees are not these superstar TED speakers or executives that these books talk about? You can't exactly come in and just clear the deck and start over with new talents, partners, vendors, and boards that fit the criteria set by those consulting books and "experts."

Modern Alchemy addresses this vacuum in a way that's unlike anything you have read before. In this book, you will learn:

- why Alchemists matter
- how to turn any lethargic group into an A-team with your existing talents and resources
- why organizational divas don't matter
- how to build credibility and get buy-in
- why some top talents cannot recreate their results after changing jobs and joining a new organization or team
- how to generate the halo effect around a group
- why trajectory and momentum matter more than culture or strategy
- how to create the FOMO (fear of missing out) effect for your organization to start to attract real talent
- how anyone can methodically acquire the Midas touch and turn any project or team into gold
- why faith and hope are important
- how to silence the noise at work
- how to create self-fulfilling prophecies
- why the right directions, role assignment, and policies beat having the world's top minds in any competition

Now the question is, how do you go from learning about Modern Alchemy... to applying its principles... to generating these results? And what about your world, what matters to you right now, and your very motivation for picking up this book? What do you have to do before you can become the go-to team, organization, company, or destination recognized locally, regionally, or internationally?

In business, the practice of Modern Alchemy means learning how to obtain and maintain magnificent results with seemingly subpar resources. When the world's top talent is unavailable or access is restricted, you can put the right systems in place to elevate your people to match and exceed the outputs and achievements expected of those deemed to be the benchmark and best in class.

To paraphrase one of America's prominent marketing consultants, Jay Abraham, it's how to "get everything you can out of all you've got." This is pure pragmatism; it is dealing with the world as it is and not as you want it to be, so that you can create the outcomes that you believe ought to be.

If change is the journey, Modern Alchemy is the map and the tool kit to see you through.

Who This Book Is For

This book is not intended to give you the full secret recipe for success, nor is it the be-all and end-all of this philosophy. It is intended to share with you a few important fundamentals, insightful tools, and examples, and to set you on your path facing the right direction.

To help the most people gain the most value from this book, I've written it with multiple tiers of readers in mind. Here is what each audience will get out of *Modern Alchemy*.

You

You are someone who understands that life and success are team sports.

You are someone who sees the benefit of collaboration, coordination, and partnering with others and the potential that opens up for everyone involved, if done correctly and if each member plays to their individual natural strengths.

You're the person in charge of an organization or project. You're in the realistic (if unfortunate) position of having few resources and a limited number of skilled talents, and yet you have to make a go of it because your livelihood, your family, and your community or team's financial security are on the line.

Unknowingly, you might even be an Alchemist or an aspiring Alchemist yourself. You'll find out through this book. Regardless, everyone around you will benefit from the knowledge you'll acquire here.

If you'd like, think of the character of Atlas from Greek mythology, who carries the weight of the world on his shoulders. In every organization, there is at least one who carries most of the load for all intents and purposes and does so willingly.

If this is you, this book will show you how to lighten the load while empowering others—without dropping your responsibilities.

Your Patrons

Any change management project must have a patron, the owner or stakeholder who believes and invests in the opportunity to move an organization from a current state to an intended future state. A patron may be an individual or a group of people, possibly even a constituency.

Patrons are the ones with the most to gain and the most to lose. It is their underlying asset, their capital, their organization, or even their country that is being "changed" to become a better version of itself.

For a patron to trust that there is a "method to the madness," we want them to be confident in the process by gaining the ability to assess change agents and the associated talents and plans. Change is difficult and painful, and patrons will always second-guess what the team is doing if they are not educated about the process, except if they know that the lead is somebody who's done this process successfully many times before.

To visualize this, think of change like emergency surgery. Imagine the seemingly chaotic scenes during surgery—the beeping heart rate monitors; blood splashing everywhere; the nurses, doctors, and technicians running in and out. But in the same scene, if you were to focus on the elements, you would notice the calm, focused, and deliberate zen-like movements of each of the specialists in the room.

Where some would see chaos and anarchy, the more informed would see the reality as it is: well-orchestrated and choreographed maneuvers. Each individual knows their role and their priority, and each knows their position within the "flock" and the chain of actions that must be taken.

When patrons understand that each individual is able, informed, and focused, trust is built, which converts into calm and continued commitment even during the seemingly chaotic chapter of the change process.

An example of this from popular culture is the English chef Gordon Ramsay and his show *Kitchen Nightmares*. He is solicited to support a fledgling restaurant by its patrons—the owners of the establishment. He walks into a restaurant and observes and analyzes the situation first, without screaming or chatting. Once he calmly assesses the elements, he restructures and reallocates responsibilities and divides up the labor, building specialization and assigning people to their unique tasks based on their abilities (e.g. this person is now in charge of the cleanliness in the kitchen, that person is now a maître d', etc.).

It's the exact same group. He doesn't recruit anybody from outside, but instead clearly draws the parameters for responsibilities and specialization from within the existing pool of resources. What he does is assess people and force them to specialize in the prioritized elements that he deems they're best at and that he deems are needed by the enterprise. He makes a few tweaks when it comes to the recipe, and then he stands back and gives it a few days to settle, possibly making a few more adjustments over time.

Needless to say, the formula works eventually, and the patron and establishment gain from the value created by the expert, by the Alchemist. The fact that this can be done over and over again proves that there is a method, a process, and a unique understanding and skill that allows for this seemingly magical conversion.

When asking a patron to risk their capital and entrust their assets to someone, patrons want to make sure that the incoming person is an Alchemist, a professional with a unique and proven skill set and track record in turning organizations around.

This book should show patrons how to start to distinguish and differentiate between the real "experts" and those "fake pseudo-expert shamans." This book should further explain to patrons what steps these change agents take to better understand the mechanisms that are followed. This is because selection is key.

The reason why selection is so important is because the selection process is all the patrons have. Once selected and once the agents are in, patrons will usually not be able to intervene or micromanage the team. Sometimes, like in the current example, they wouldn't even be at liberty to ask, "Why have that person as maître d' as opposed to someone else?" They have no choice but to trust the incoming "expert" and the process.

This is simply because a true change agent will simply pick up and leave if he is offended by interference—and rightly so. He's got hundreds, thousands, even millions of other potential patrons, problems, or companies he could be turning around and has limited time to waste on educating laymen. He has respect and confidence in his ability and demands that any assessment of his work is made based on the final outcome.

He takes full responsibility for the process and the outcome and therefore must be provided room to maneuver.

Patrons need to understand this reality if they are to attract and retain real change agents who can create value for them and their enterprise. This book will help them gain trust in the process.

We want patrons to have an opportunity to understand the role of Alchemists, to understand how to best identify them, and to start to have confidence in Alchemists and their abilities. If the Alchemists can validate that they know what they're doing, the patron can then step back from operational decision-making and trust that the outcome will be to their benefit.

Your Talent

For talents in an organization, this book provides invaluable insights.

This is because what talents need is very different from the needs of patrons. Talents do not need to develop confidence in their ability to select change agents to follow. What they really require is the ability to identify an opportunity to join the right group and be part of something great—to commit to a marching and growing tribe.

To do that effectively, talents must learn to assess leaders and change agents and to be able to weigh the viability of the direction being taken. They must be able to check the organization's ultimate ability to play to the talents' strengths.

When done right, when the talent joins the right group and commits, the outcome is life-changing.

You see, what they really need is the ability to pierce through the narrative. They need to know if this Alchemist truly knows what he's doing. They need to know if this group can survive challenges and build momentum. They need to know if this group can take off and reach the escape velocity required for greatness.

Only then would the talent be able to have faith in the future prospects of the group, organization, team, or corporation. And only then would the talents perform at the absolute highest level and commit fully.

Sometimes, finding an Alchemist or a group to join is not so dramatic. Sometimes, it's not so loud. Sometimes, it's much more nuanced and much less in your face.

This is why talents need to acquire the skill to pick the right leader to commit to.

One piece of advice that I always repeat is, "Follow, lead, or get out of the way." It's my version of a famously used phrase. I start with "follow" purposefully. My advice is always to start by finding a good and able leader to follow and serve. Only when such a leader is nowhere to be found should someone try to lead. Most of the time, your value add is greater in the second, third, and fourth tiers, not always up in the front.

Be the reluctant leader, I say. Do this, and you and your group will reach unexpected heights.

I appreciate it is counterintuitive to hear emphasis on the benefit of following and supporting a group in an age where every consultant, high school teacher, and book espouses leadership and individualism. We have reached a point where every individual is deemed to be or aspires to be a "leader" and there are no followers. This is simply illogical if the aim is greater accomplishments. Solo does not always cut it.

The reality of the matter is that the wise follow. Think about the teams within the Tour de France, and think about the image of a flock of geese flying. In both, the followers benefit while the leader faces the highest resistance and carries the highest load. In both, the leader is reluctant and needs support from the back.

Therefore, it is my opinion that the wise follow and only step up to the plate for the benefit of the group or the organization when there is no one more able to lead.

Everyone Else

As for the masses, this book is designed to provoke a readiness to revisit and reassess old customs and assumptions. It's meant to get conversations going about what we can do and how we can do it, with examples we've tried, problems we've solved, and tools and tips we've picked up along the way.

The masses are what gives the process its aura, what I call the halo effect. They don't need to understand the method exactly, but they have hope that change is possible. They've seen the potential, and their hope and faith levitate the team.

For them, this book explains some of the principles and techniques that make it happen. And by "it," I'm referring to turning something of nominal value into something sought after.

Not a How-To

Note that this is not a how-to book or a recipe book in the linear sense (Step 1, Step 2, Step 3, etc.). Yes, I explain general principles and provide a few introductory techniques, and yes, there are some activities that one does in a particular logical order. But you need to appreciate that Modern Alchemy as introduced in this book is more a craft than a set of instructions. There are components, there are systems, and there is a philosophy. Some are done in a given sequence, others are done in parallel, but all are learned through trial and practice, and all require an Alchemist.

So, let's get started.

Who I Am and Why I Wrote This Book

I have been lucky. Serendipity has been good to me. My story is one that only God could write.

I've had the unique opportunity to work with some amazing people in ever-greater change projects, each generating an even larger ripple. In many projects, I followed incredible leaders to whom I'm eternally grateful, and in more recent endeavors, I led some brilliant talents and made a difference. And in all, I learned, took copious notes, and systemized, iterating as we went along.

Our teams have done many great things that I'm very proud of, some even seemingly impossible tasks and projects. And in all, we brought about a change and added value.

I started the journey as a small entrepreneur with a handful of partners, finding niches where we could add value and positively disrupt specific sectors for the benefit of our clients and customers.

I then moved on to becoming a litigator, where I focused with my colleagues on "righting wrongs," serving and helping the underdogs in facing their nightmares and their bullies, an immensely fulfilling role.

The projects then naturally moved into the realm of consulting, building, and molding commercial institutions, where we combined talents from different expertise and backgrounds to solve problems and create value for our patrons.

Naturally, this evolved into supporting patrons in acquiring subpar commercial organizations, recalibrating them and turning them around, creating value where there was none—or some.

The final element was to support the local ecosystem, where I took on a role as a government cabinet minister (the youngest at the time) to focus on supporting the adoption of policies that benefited the realm, creating an open, competitive, and just ecosystem. My focus was on "synthesizing hope" for a youthful population, be it through supporting the designing the education reforms strategy; creating a performance-driven sports sector; developing a youth-focused venture capital arm; injecting predictability and reliability within the system; or developing the first media brand that focuses on startup and growth capital opportunities—all efforts that have created opportunities for and touched the lives of many within the constituency.

I am no longer a cabinet minister but instead focus on supporting my patrons and the community by supervising change projects in the youth and sports sector, and through serving on the boards of a number of organizations that I'm proud to be associated with.

There is a tremendous amount of overlap in the learning that took place and in the teams that I worked with every step of the way. There are key lessons that I share and stand by:

- Life is a team sport. Nothing is achieved alone.

- Life is a multi-generational sport.

- Long-term, repetitive, voluntary, trust-based interactions and relationships with acquired depth trump and are much more beneficial and efficient in the long term than transient, transactional, one-off interactions. Note that many of the people I serve with today were there at the very beginning.

- Noise and celebrations are very rarely a bad thing.

Looking back, the one shared, underlying theme in everything that we've done relates to change and change management, value creation at its most fundamental. Our teams worked tirelessly to take situations from their "current state" to their preferred "intended future state."

And on the way, we had to build our own tools and methods. We institutionalized the learning to allow for repetition and scale, and it worked like a charm.

As with all projects, we wanted to change a current state that did not take too kindly to change. Fortunately, we documented the alchemical approach, and after many failed attempts, we refined our craft.

Looking back now, I wish we had this book or something like it prior to all that! If someone had written about how to plan and execute, how to perform, how to turn around an organization or a team with very limited resources, both human and financial, and to do so with minimal disruption, I'd have read it in a heartbeat. And I would have saved so much time and effort that was wasted being allocated to low-impact, high-resistance efforts.

If we had that book, we would have gotten here sooner.

The benefit is that you now have this book to help you and your organization jumpstart your change journey.

Audit Your Hypothesis

1. Are you ready to learn Modern Alchemy and temporarily suspend your previous misconceptions about organizational leadership and change management? Yes ☐ No ☐

2. Do you know who you are reading this book for? (You, your patrons, your talent, or the general public?) Yes ☐ No ☐

3. Do you know your current state and your future intended state? Yes ☐ No ☐

4. Do you understand that Modern Alchemy could mean making drastic changes to your current business leadership approach? Yes ☐ No ☐

5. Do you get that sometimes, the highest value you can provide is by following and supporting and not by leading? Yes ☐ No ☐

CHAPTER 2

THE ALCHEMIST

There is no alchemy without an Alchemist. There is no change without the change agent. He, or she, is the single most important variable in the equation.

So taking the time to get the selection of the Alchemist right is more important than any other part of the transformation process. Fail in the selection process, fail in scouting, and fail in retaining the Alchemist, and there will be no gold.

What's the Big Deal about Alchemists?

Understanding Their Potential

If the purpose of the exercise or the effort you're undertaking is to change something mediocre into something great, to raise a group or an organization to far exceed the sum of its parts, then finding and selecting the Alchemist is a very big deal. It is crucial. Without this individual, there will be no transformation.

Let me give you a metaphor that can help visualize the truth of the matter. Think of yeast.

Yeast

(noun)

- a microscopic fungus consisting of single oval cells that reproduce by budding, and are capable of converting sugar into alcohol and carbon dioxide

Think of the simple act of baking bread. You mix together your ingredients—your flour, your water, your salt, and so forth—but you leave out the yeast. You put the mix in the oven at the designated temperature. It heats up, and it even cooks, but it does not rise.

On completion, you end up with a deflated product, a fraction of the size and quality you expected. It is nothing compared to what it could have been or should have been, had it been done properly.

The size of the product at the end, when it's all said and done, equates to the sum of the contents you placed into the mix—the sum of its parts.

Now, imagine repeating the same procedure exactly, but this time you add one more element; you sprinkle a pinch of yeast—the tiny material between your fingertips that seemingly cannot possibly impact the overall size of that loaf. But then, like magic, something happens. In the oven, the loaf rises.

What changed between the first attempt and the second? The only variable was a sprinkle of yeast.

That's the impact of yeast; that's the impact of an Alchemist. With it, when added to the mix, the product becomes greater than the sum of its parts. Everything rises.

I would argue that an Alchemist's impact on an organization, a project, a community or a cause is similar to the impact visibly seen from yeast. Alchemists make the whole greater—or look greater—than the sum. They create additional value where there was none—or some.

When an organization has an Alchemist, the output of individuals within the organization seems to increase. The quality of products and services becomes better. The innovation and drive of working teams rise. Profitability rises. Everyone performs better. Everybody benefits. And what's more, previously unknown talents and gems get identified and empowered to play better and bigger roles. You find that everyone's game rises within the organization. What's more, the performance of competing and collaborating organizations and teams also rises. The ripple effect is incredible.

Alchemists raise the bar. They raise expectations, and they raise everyone with them. They are the secret ingredient. They're the game changers.

Simply put, Alchemists are what you add to an orchestra, and seemingly miraculously, they produce symphonies. Add them to a sports team, and almost magically, you have a winning franchise producing superstars, a loyal following, and merchandise. It's the same when it comes to universities, hospitals, governments, or any other body. Just one or two of these key individuals with the necessary knowledge and skills raises the whole immediate ecosystem.

There is a legendary story about Steve Jobs that beautifully sums up the role of Alchemists within an organization. It is said that during a dispute, Steve Wozniak had told Steve Jobs, "You can't write code. You're not an engineer. You're not a designer.

You can't put a hammer to a nail. What do you do?" Steve Jobs's answer was eloquent and clear. He said, "I play the orchestra,"[1] referring to his role in organizing the talents, guiding the talent, pushing the talents, setting the standard, understanding and playing to individual members' strengths, and building harmony.

Having now been introduced to the concept, there is no doubt that names come to mind from every industry—names of individuals that when included in a roster in a team, company, or project, the overall performance of the whole is visibly amplified without changing any of the other individuals or the financial resources at hand.

The impact of these individuals over time becomes so recognizable that some start to be referred to as "lucky," "gifted," and sometimes even "superhuman." Some even join the ranks of mythology.

If you look at the Titans and the Olympians, the so-called "gods" or "demi-gods" of ancient Greece, you'll notice that they are spoken of in a way similar to how, in the States, they speak of the Founding Fathers, or kings and titans of industry like the Vanderbilts, the Carnegies, the Rothschilds, or the Rockefellers—and in closer times, Elon Musk, Steve Jobs, and Jeff Bezos. In the art of governance, you hear similar echoes and similar nuances in stories about the Medicis of Florence, King Louis XIV of France, Lee Kuan Yew of Singapore, or Sheikh Mohammed bin Rashid Al Maktoum of Dubai. This goes even further in history, reaching to pharaohs and finally even Arthur and his Camelot.

I have always thought that these individuals may have simply been Alchemists—having gained the skill to levitate the community and people around them, to solve problems and add

---

[1] *Steve Jobs,* directed by Danny Boyle (2015; Universal Pictures).

value—creating this halo effect over time until it reached a silly point where their reputations simply transcended mortal form through repetition of their achievements over the ages.

What is important for this context is the hypothesis that this skill, the skill to turn mediocrity into magnificence, was learned—regardless if legends were eventually made. And if the skill was learned, then it may be acquired, and it may be taught.

And more importantly, if individuals with the skill exist, then they may be identified and may be recruited.

What If the Alchemist Leaves?

I hope you're now convinced that one individual can positively impact an entity or community and cause a ripple effect that changes everything. If so, I would like to invite you to consider a matter that is essential in understanding the importance of Alchemists, particularly when considering the yeast metaphor and its impact on organizations or even whole jurisdictions.

Consider this. If it is true that Alchemists, like yeast, raise their surroundings, positively impacting their colleagues and all that they interact with—yielding exponentially ever-growing returns and benefits for all—what happens if one day they leave?

It seems clear from observations that the positive impact which they create is not everlasting and only lasts for as long as they continue to be there and are engaged. Very soon after they leave, the organization is no longer greater than the sum of its parts. Instead, it simply goes back to being merely equal to the sum of its parts and, at times, continues its downward trajectory.

I appreciate that sometimes, the effect of the departure is not felt instantaneously. I have come across a number of examples where the downward trajectory may be interrupted at times by embedding protocols and putting rigid processes in place. But that amounts to nothing more than muscle memory. It is at par with body parts continuing to twitch and grow for a short period after the heart has stopped while the soul and life of the individual have long departed. The overall becomes but a shell and a shadow of its past. In other words, when yeast leaves, the bread deflates. Imagine that.

We've seen this example repeat itself time after time in a wide variety of sectors, be they in government, corporations, not-for-profits, sports teams, or others.

Let me give you some imagery that might better illustrate the point and ensure the acceptance of the proposition. Think of countries that have gone through abrupt, if short-lived, violent revolutions. Upon the commencement of a violent revolution and just before borders are closed indefinitely, a small percentage of the population, usually some of the most enlightened and high-impact of the skilled labor force and those who abhor violence and force, quietly make their way out of the country.

We have all seen examples of destinations that are simply a shell of their glorious past, more archeological sites now than a city. When walking through those roads and cities amongst monumental man-made structures, it sometimes seems as if the whole population simply got up and walked away.

But the reality, I would suggest, is much slower than that. The reality is that when Alchemists leave, the community starts to wither away. It is a slow deterioration culminating in a zombie-like state. This applies to all types of organizations and all types of groups, corporations, institutions, teams, and even states.

Now, if these observations stand correct, then logic dictates that these Alchemists are more than just important.

Alchemists as National Treasures

I have had the distinct privilege of being able to work on some incredible projects so far in my professional career, some catered to teams, others to corporations, and some even catered to the needs of nations. And during this time, I have come to a realization from my interactions with Alchemists.

The same way that Alchemists or yeast can raise an organization or a community, they can just as readily deflate an organization with the very simple and yet extremely potent act of disengaging and stepping away, an action I refer to in my lexicon as "podiacracy"—voting with your feet.

When countries publish reports and assessments by their national security strategists, they usually identify the risk of "brain drain" among their highest concerns. This "brain drain" is not always organic; sometimes, it occurs due to targeted solicitation through the extension of opportunities by competing forces. We will revisit brain drain again in upcoming sections.

Now, if the premise is correct, and if external groups are scoping Alchemists that reside within their competitors' rosters, then it would logically be fair to conclude that these Alchemists are assets—at times, national assets, and therefore, national treasures.

The same, of course, applies in the realm of business or any other sector, as corporate multinationals, too, consider talent flight or migration as one of their highest risks.

Therefore, identifying, empowering, appreciating, and supporting Alchemists should be at the core of any group, community, company, or nation's strategy.

Now ask yourself this: Do you track your Alchemists? Do you cater to your Alchemists? Do you attract Alchemists? Do you empower and incentivize your Alchemists?

Do You Know Your Alchemists?

Having established that Alchemists are assets and treasures that should not be taken for granted, the key is identifying them early on whether internally or externally and enticing their interests in the projects or purpose for which your group or organization is created.

Of all the projects that I have had the privilege to work on, none of the steps are as positively impactful to organizations or to communities as the focus on creating institutional talent scouting and grooming systems and identifying their strength. It is suggested that this will always be the first thing that any alchemist would do upon taking over a mandate. Any organization, team, or state that does not give absolute priority to talent identification and eventually the search for and discovery of alchemists is a lost cause, in my view. They have lost even before they have started.

There are a few discrete traits and characteristics that stand out in Alchemists that help the wise in readily identifying them, allowing them to stand out of the crowd.

I'll share a few with you, but this is in no way a comprehensive list. This is meant to give a taste only; scouting Alchemists is a skill that requires lifelong obsession.

Not Every Smart Person Is an Alchemist

When experts talk about national security strategies in *any* country, they might also refer to their fear of "brain drain"—the exit of high-performing individuals from their country of origin. Multinational organizations from startups to multibillion-dollar corporations claim they have to "compete for talent."

What does this mean? I believe that they are not simply talking about IQ; they're talking about individuals with refined skills and abilities. They're talking about the mobilization, migration, and activation of Alchemists. Because without their contributions to the community, the whole eventually deflates.

That said, I think that the use of the word "brain" in "brain drain" might be a misnomer and may not clearly present to readers the traits of the persons being referenced. I believe that this may have thrown people off the real concept for quite some time.

"Brain drain" seems to give the connotation that organizations or countries should track individuals who are simply "smart," arguably with an IQ or G factor higher than the average. But having worked for years with many local, regional, and international counterparts the world over on this specific subject, I can confirm that the traits in question are not simply smarts.

You'll appreciate that there are a lot of extremely smart people out there that neither impact nor benefit their surroundings. Think of the individuals you've heard about with maddeningly high IQs and photographic memories, but who live in a cocoon, unfettered and undisturbed by reality. This is not an Alchemist.

Intelligence is not enough, although smarts do play a role. "Smart" is simply the bandwidth that an individual has, which is a genetically inherited ability. But just because someone has the ability or the skill does not mean that they activate it or that they have refined it—or, for that matter, put it to good use.

As a simple metaphor, the higher the IQ or G factor, the higher one can see over the horizon and the higher up one's head rises over the others. The problem with that concept is that eventually, one reaches a point where one's head is "simply in the clouds," dealing with conceptual mental models that no one on the ground can relate to, nor do they have any real application.

The reason one refers to "heads in the clouds" is because of the obsessive nature of the Alchemists. If they have a puzzle to solve, they are like "dogs with a bone," unable to move on until this has been squared in their mental models.

So Alchemists live not in the clouds but in the very specific sweet spot where they have their heads in the clouds, yes, but they also have their feet squarely on the ground; where they deal with mental models and make incredible observations but then experiment with their implementation.

More importantly, Alchemists are individuals who impact their communities and surroundings positively and whose existence within a community or organization raises the whole. These are not individuals living a solitary existence; they are not recluses. They are embedded within their surroundings spending seemingly illogical amounts of time focusing on adding value to their surroundings.

For visualization purposes, imagine them to be a gardener walking around cautiously watering and adding soil and nutrients to plants around themselves, at times moving whole plants to allow greater access to sunlight and, therefore, a higher potential of a perfect blossom.

It is for this reason that when scouting for Alchemists, you're looking for individuals with a strong intellect but not such high self-admiration or high-minded ideas that their heads get into the clouds. We need their feet squarely on the ground. We want them not to be too introverted so that they enjoy working with people, but they must be introspective. They should have higher conscientiousness, which includes an obsessive streak. They should be low in agreeableness and very open to questioning everything and revisiting previous dogmas. They should not be too neurotic or else they would exhaust themselves and everyone around them.

In other words, la-la land does not cut it. And one thing is for sure: Alchemists are not simply talent.

Sadly, Alchemists are not always loud. Actually, they're quite the opposite—they have no real sign of narcissistic, psychopathic, tyrannical leaders that tend to signal the existence of some sad inferiority complexes. Alchemists tend not to have any of that because of their ability, which allows them to be calmer and more controlled.

Then how can you spot the work of an Alchemist? Take a step back and look for ripple effects. Work your way back to the middle, and I guarantee that you'll find an Alchemist.

Alchemists Bring Back Good News

Another clear way to identify an Alchemist is the news that they bring back to the patron. There is a phrase that one uses when soldiers go off on a mission that is a favorite of mine and seems to fit the context here:

"Come back with good news."

The "come back" element is simple. It's a wish that the forces being dispatched stay safe, mitigate risks, and make it back soon to take their place within their families and communities. It's a reminder that undue risk is unnecessary and should not be taken lightly. The "with good news" element is almost a condition for reintegration into the community as returning champions or "victors," considering what that means to the community's security and their livelihoods.

We are all grateful for the service and the extreme sacrifices of our men and women in uniform, each in their respective jurisdictions. And we are even prouder of their disciplined states of mind in always focusing on "coming back with good news."

Alchemists have the same level of conscientiousness. They, too, feel shame when returning back to a patron or patrons, beneficiaries of the Alchemist's skills, with bad news—worse yet when presenting an excuse.

Therefore, it's simple. If someone comes back with excuses on why he failed on a mission, he is not an Alchemist—because an Alchemist would not have given up and would not have come back, or, better yet, would never have undertaken the challenge had they not been convinced.

An Alchemist, therefore, does not hedge and does not return without a proverbial "victory" and would feel shame if he did. The only reason an Alchemist would be seen in "barracks" would be if he has yet to leave, has been summoned back and removed from a commission, or has returned with a victory.

Think about the number of times you have heard that "it should not be possible." Half, if not all, of David Goggins's feats should not be possible. The four-minute mile should not be possible. We see, the world over and on a daily basis, impossible challenges being relegated to the category of "simply difficult." The formula is simple: Give it everything, leave nothing behind, and truly embody the "victory or death" calls.

And usually, there's an Alchemist spearheading the quest for the impossible. They are usually the ones that "think differently," that are the "crazy ones," the ones that see opportunity where others see barriers.

Remember that I'm referring here not to the actual task at hand or the fact that it was achieved. I'm referring to the fact that it was deemed "impossible" before these individuals demoted them to "possible but difficult."

Interestingly enough, people that have that spirit and willingness to "leave it on the table" tend to bring the same tenacity to their projects. (See Goggins's experience in writing his self-published #1 bestseller, again an "impossible" task marked as done.)

So, to conclude: An Alchemist, once launched, would not willingly and freely come back without a "mission accomplished." If a candidate does not show that, he's not an Alchemist. Simple.

Alchemists Never Touch the Ball

The key challenge in identifying Alchemists is that they're almost never where you would assume them to be, meaning they're almost never where the action is taking place.

Let's revisit this concept. The Alchemist is the chef, or coach, or conductor. But not like the single outlet chefs; more like a chef overseeing a global network of operations. There's a big difference. The single-unit chef has no real conceptualization of what he's doing because he can't formulate it and institutionalize it, evidenced by the fact that he's in the kitchen. The multi-unit chef understands his craft to such a level that he can embed his "way" for the product to be generated even when he's not physically there.

Therefore, an Alchemist is never, ever a musician; he's never carrying the actual instrument. The Alchemist is never, ever a player, so you won't find him running up and down the field with the ball while crowds go mad. Pick any metaphor. Alchemists always appear to be standing on the sidelines and (more impressively) the truly gifted Alchemists don't appear at all. They're not in the action; they're not in the huddle. They're not on the pitch; they're not on the stage.

That's an Alchemist in a nutshell.

They are the storytellers. They are the fortune tellers. They are the narrative builders. They select the destination and the team, and they manage the distribution of the spoils of victory. But they are never, ever executives and never active on the field.

But one must also remember who Alchemists must contend with—shareholders and stakeholders, and at times, a whole community of constituents. These are, at times, people who want to feel in control. It is very common to see such uninformed, unskilled individuals asking questions, providing guidelines, issuing orders, and providing advice or instructions in an attempt to participate in the change exercise. The reality is that this is as productive as sports viewers shouting instructions at a TV screen during a game: not productive at all.

On a more humorous note, attempts to interfere in the Alchemist's work sometimes remind me of an episode of *The Simpsons*. While the mother, Marge, is driving, her little daughter Maggie has her own little steering wheel, turning it this way and that, thinking she is steering. She—and the uniformed stakeholder—wants to be pandered to and wants to feel involved in the decision-making process . . . despite that in doing so, she does not add any value.

It's very rare for an Alchemist to allow such intervention, although I have seen a few young Alchemists give immature stakeholders or clients Maggie Simpson's fake steering wheel to feel as if they are supporting the process. The attempt backfires every time. It's best to set clear boundaries from the very beginning.

Wise Alchemists know to shut out such interventions regardless of whom they come from and to make that a condition of their engagement. Either the Alchemist is leading or someone else is leading. There is no sharing the wheel or the burden.

It is true that Alchemists take full responsibility for the mandate, but that does not mean that they do all the work or even that they do someone else's work. Remember that Alchemists are playing the orchestra and are not members of the orchestra.

The best symbolism I found over the years is that of coaches. The best sports coaches make it clear that you **cannot** pass the ball to them during the game (obviously). They're part of the team, but they're not on the field—and rightly so.

But these wise Alchemists or coaches understand, like the best army generals, that at first contact, all previous plans and assumptions are out the window. It is only staff selection, preparation, positioning, training, intelligence, coordination, incentivization, empowerment, strategy, and intuition that matters.

Think about it for a second. A skipper on a sailboat is never running around the boat; he is always looking across the horizon or eyeing operations. A good coach is never running on the field; a composer is never on the stage; a producer is never on the set or the screen; a statesman doesn't deal with the operation of the state apparatus; an engineer does not mix the concrete nor set the stones; a master planner does not clear the roads. But without them, nothing would be done and there would be no completion.

So it is with Alchemists. The Alchemist's work is completed long before first contact. During game time, they don't do much.

They don't do anything at all. Their job was completed long before. They do not interrupt the execution, but they do decide what resources to throw at different situations in the future based on the learning from this interaction.

Remember that Alchemists play the long game, the infinite one, understanding that the outcome of one skirmish or one interaction is never the end goal. Alchemists think systematically and methodically. They do not bark individual discretionary orders nor play politics; they tweak the system and change the algorithms. They amend the organizational charts and change the allocation of resources, but they're never wasting precious time and energy deciding on the threads used in team uniforms nor the tiles to be used in the construction of team bathrooms, nor do they interfere in the selection of the team's bus. But they do select the people that make these decisions. They watch them closely, set the parameters to guide them to success, and ensure that they incentivize them correctly. Simply put, Alchemists are never operational.

Alchemists understand the levers that they have, and they use them and only them to get to the intended future state. These levers do not include intervention in individual tasks. What is the point of dealing with individual items when you know that you have a stream of items coming out of a conveyor belt? You need to find the defect within the machine and never fix individual, commoditized products.

Alchemists Build Dams

The previous section does not imply that the temptation to get embroiled in day-to-day goings-on isn't there. It very much is.

For even the greatest Alchemists, it's a challenge in avoiding getting sucked into daily operations. This is simply a muscle that one needs to strengthen. The wisest Alchemists have the foresight to build proverbial dams to protect their focus on the end goal from a flood of unnecessary tasks boomeranged back to them from time to time.

Think of it this way: Alchemists follow a similar prioritization model to Jeff Bezos. The Amazon founder stated at times that he does not work on guiding any project that is less than twelve years away from rollout. Therefore, he is not dealing with the here and now because his real job is to imagine, create, and deliver a future state.

Because Modern Alchemy demands a singular focus on the future, I will explain further. Alchemists do not boomerang and do not accept boomerangs. When an Alchemist is given an organization to turn around, the delegated task will never return to the patron requesting intervention. Similarly, the diced and delegated tasks will not come back to Alchemists from their subordinates; Alchemists won't accept them. They do not participate in the decision-making at the individual task level; they select individuals to handle such matters.

Consider this real-life simple boomerang example. When you hire someone to wash your vehicle, they shouldn't ask you repeatedly for your attention, feedback, or approval. "What kind of soap do you want me to use? In what direction do you want me to scrub the vehicle?" That's not what Alchemists do. The car simply comes back clean; that's simply how Alchemists are.

Thankfully, this reality makes the job of experienced Alchemist scouts much easier. It allows them to cross off the list any candidates who are seen barking—or, in this day and age, messaging—orders to anyone who needs to be present in all meetings and anyone interfering in the decision-making process of subordinates while questioning and critiquing everything. Simply put, they remove any of the nano-managers—the next generation of micromanagers.

These are not Alchemists and will not be able to raise the whole. They will simply become the selfish bottlenecks that hold back progress.

Another simple, visible giveaway is time allocation and the generosity in allocating time. Does the person have time? Are they altruistically generous in its allocation, or is it treated as the most precious of fleeting commodities? If the person does not have time to do the high-priority items that they believe they need to, they're not Alchemists. They're too hands-on, and they're stuck in the quicksand.

Later in the book, we'll go over the tools that the Alchemist uses to build the dam to keep at bay the upward tsunami of requests and boomerangs they receive from misplaced talents. This will explain how it is that the Alchemist can safeguard against being beyond drowned in the minutia of operational issues.

My argument is that all companies or organizations need to have one individual—a leader, a sort of choreographer or conductor—who keeps everyone facing the right direction. That's all it takes to change the whole proposition of the organization. You see, every ship has a skipper, who is the ultimate arbiter of its direction and the ultimate architect of its future; he is the ship's Alchemist. You can only have one—and he must be selected by the patron and granted room to do his "magic."

Now, let's review an Alchemist's key traits.

Alchemist Qualities Checklist

- Never has operational roles
- Can only work with full autonomy
- Displays a strategic problem-solving ability
- Is committed to systems and processes
- Is committed to continuous iterative progress
- Is purposeful and careful in allocating time
- Is decisive and responsible
- Refuses to micromanage, let alone nano-manage
- Thinks in big pictures and plays the infinite, indefinite game
- Builds dams to prevent distractions
- Never, ever drops the ball willingly
- Never, ever does anyone else's work and never allows others to do it either, because it weakens the whole
- Gets the job or mandate done

Now that you understand what an Alchemist is and how to recognize them, let's transition to what they do in practice. Every Alchemist begins the organization's transformational change journey with the future in mind. That does not mean they have a goal or even a specific destination or end in mind. In the next chapter, you'll learn why that matters—and what Alchemists do instead.

Audit Your Alchemy

1. Can you clearly understand and identify who is an alchemist? Yes ☐ No ☐

2. Do you understand the impact of alchemists on nations, organizations, or business environments? Yes ☐ No ☐

3. Do you understand the importance of alchemists?
   Yes ☐ No ☐

4. Can you identify alchemists by their qualities and traits?
   Yes ☐ No ☐

CHAPTER 3

THE DIRECTION

Modern Alchemy, when done properly, offers an amazing paradigm shift at every level of your organization—from setting the company mission to employee compensation, from selecting senior leadership to indoctrinating new interns.

The one element that Alchemists understand better than others is that they are playing an infinite game, one with no end in sight. The approach and the state of mind therefore must be completely different. With an infinite mindset, you focus on a direction, a Due North, and you iterate continuously to get closer to your intended outcome. The game changer here is that even if the environmental or external elements change, you would still be able to comfortably iterate, self-correct, and continue on.

With a finite mindset on the other hand, one has a set destination and a set route; any changes in plans or environment would make the execution of the plan impossible, considering the changed variables.

To clarify the difference, with a finite perspective, one focuses on individual battles as if they are ends. An infinite perspective, meanwhile, teaches us to be selective in allocating resources and investing energy. It teaches us to prioritize what matters when it comes to the overall outcome.

A focus on direction instead of destination reconfigures your mind about what matters. It argues that the most important thing in an organization is not to build a shared culture or publish a business or project plan, as is proposed by advisers the world over in this day and age. The most important thing is the organization's shared direction, the focus on the trajectory and increasing the momentum, therefore granting the organization an infinite goal as opposed to a finite destination.

Simply put, detailed plans set out and locked in from the beginning, showing the step-by-step task list and their dependencies leading to a predefined static end state, leads to failure every single time, especially when one is playing an infinite, indefinite game. An attempt to plan and author an organization's future with all its intricate details simply does not work. The reality is that there are an infinite number of variables and an infinite number of unknowns that are constantly changing and evolving and, better yet, being impacted by internal and external forces. There is no way that anyone can honestly predict an exact future.

I don't want to sound nihilistic nor passive; I am simply realistic and pragmatic. Drawing the route to an exact, static future state predefined in time and place is beyond what anyone can do. That's a fact. But what we can easily do and do well is define the direction in which one should head.

The idea is simple: Never set a "North Star"—a fixed destination. Instead, decide on a direction, a "Due North" which you can aspire to follow. This is a key differentiator between Alchemists and simple managers. Alchemists understand that there is no fixed destination and that therefore the journey is continuous and never-ending, which requires preparation, strategic allocation of resources, and pacing. Others burn out eventually because they are only ready for a quick sprint.

Setting a direction and trajectory allows one to continue to iterate and course-correct continuously, designing the system to cater to the many unexpected bumps on the way, but never interrupting the journey. When considered in that manner, even the worst surprises do not interrupt the forward movement toward the future, even if one is temporarily off course at times.

Therefore, any real comprehensive effort to fix an organization that's broken must start with this reality in mind: An organization has limited resources and is made to last an eternity, so the priority is always to make iterative changes for the better while safeguarding its sustainability and protecting its longevity. One way to do it is to always try to discover and refine the answer to the question, "What do we need more of?" This will start to unwrap the real direction.

I appreciate that you've probably read that effective goal-setting and effective budgeting leads to success in the boardroom, at home, and everywhere else. This is a foundational belief many academic advisors hold. I would suggest from experience that it's wrong. I argue that their adherence to targets is misguided and, more importantly, inefficient in the long run.

In this chapter, you should experience a mindset shift that may at first feel counterintuitive but then settle in quite comfortably, because what is being proposed naturally exists within the praxeological nature of man. We all move toward safer spaces and away from danger; toward comfort and away from discomfort; toward opportunity and away from servitude; toward wealth and away from poverty; toward knowledge and away from naivete.

And organizations are nothing but a group of people. And so, naturally, the group, through its individual members, would always march toward more of one thing and away from its inverse.

Think about it for a second. Here is a sample list of "directions" that I've worked on over the years:

> What do we need from education? More skills that increase prospects of employability?
>
> What do we need from youth services? More hope?
>
> What do we need from justice and the rule of law? More predictability?
>
> What do we need from markets? More opportunity?
>
> What do we need from states? More safety?
>
> What would you want from a litigation firm? More wins?

If the need is clear, the direction is clear. And if the direction is clear, you can start to build momentum, one step at a time.

Let me share a story with you so you can see what I mean.

A "Gold Only" Organization

From 2018, I was honored to serve as the minister for youth and sports affairs in my birthplace, the Kingdom of Bahrain. The organization and the ecosystem had very good, well-meaning, able individuals, each working to pull the organization forward, but each in their own direction, as per set project plans.

Even with all the incredible effort invested by everyone and all the selfless service that was being put in, we were going nowhere.

Imagine a tug of war between well-meaning groups, each marching in the opposite direction. Worse yet, imagine many crossing ropes, many interconnected, three-dimensional tugs-of-war going on simultaneously. Even with all that energy, the organization seemed paralyzed.

We were all over the place, each on his or her own treadmill, putting in a herculean effort, but we were simply not moving. It was an exhausting state of affairs for all, regardless of how well-meaning we all were. Time and resources were being expended right, left, and center with no real lasting impact.

Project managers diligently opened individual projects while reacting to whatever was trending that week or reacting to an emergency that came up. They would set tasks for us all and help herd us toward random targets. This really did feel like running on a treadmill.

We were trying to be all things to all people. We were trying to do it all. We were failing, and everyone felt it.

Once we realized we were getting nowhere, we stopped in the most literal sense and asked ourselves, "What do we really want to accomplish? What is it that we want more of?" We had endless strategy sessions, all well meaning, all long, and yet, still nothing.

This all changed one day when His Highness Sh. Nasser bin Hamad Al Khalifa, our youth and sports patron who needs no introduction, gave an off-the-cuff speech at an event presided over by His Majesty the King of Bahrain, in which he stated that Bahrain is not only going for gold but wants "gold only" from its participation in sports events.

This was the epiphany we were all waiting for. It fit perfectly. We now had a direction.

Over the next few weeks, we went through a complete audit and realignment of the system. We were going for "gold only," and anything that wasn't pushing or pulling us in that direction would be cut out. As for financial incentives, everything was tweaked to focus on "gold only."

Overnight, we adopted a performance-driven approach. We now had our Due North, and every director, manager, supervisor, and team member was to realign as much as possible in that direction. We wanted to come back in first place (i.e., carrying the gold) in as many of the events that we participated in as possible. Yet all of us had to figure out how to bring us close to "gold only."

Once you've decided it's "gold only," everything else follows. Everything falls into place.

We were no longer celebrating attempts or efforts. That was clear. We weren't going for silvers or bronzes or a total number of medals. That was the past; we were now "gold only."

For the first time, the metrics we needed to track for each individual, federation, and directorate became crystal clear. Everybody had to justify resource allocation based on the gold-only program premise. And the beauty of it was, instead of spending our energy in a carpet-bombing approach scattering efforts all over the place, we were suddenly all rowing in the same direction.

Soon after, it was clear to all to see who of us and which programs were moving the needle and who were not. Diagnosis is more than half the battle. The next step was to minimize the waste of resources. We were getting better each day, and everyone could feel it. Momentum was building.

This all culminated in the Arabian Gulf Cup, a popular football (soccer) tournament in our region. Bahrain has competed since the first event decades ago but was not able to win first place. Great efforts were made and much money was spent, but we never came back with gold.

Many in the ministry and within the country were so frustrated that some of us literally wondered if our efforts were jinxed. One of the weird, funny, popular superstitions at the time was that the supporter's footwear needed to be turned upside down during the game. We were desperate. We laughed about it—and quietly and secretly turned the footwear over. Needless to say, it didn't work.

This all changed with the realignment program. It finally happened for the first time since 1970: Bahrain's national football team won gold and brought back the cup at the twenty-fourth Arabian Gulf Cup. The response was electrifying. Our team had done it. The supposed curse was broken.

The impact of this focus extended beyond football. Bahrain's national handball team advanced to the 2024 Paris Olympics after an inspiring performance in the Asian qualifiers, defeating strong regional rivals. Our basketball team also shone, securing victory in the prestigious GCC tournament. The momentum continued to build, culminating in Bahrain's best-ever performance at the 2024 Paris Olympics, where the kingdom ranked first among Arab nations and thirty-third globally.

These triumphs across multiple sports show the long-term effects of our "gold only" mentality. By focusing our energy and resources on excellence, we have not only uplifted our national sports but also placed Bahrain firmly on the global stage as a competitive force.

Instead of considering multiple, potential directions, we identified those one or two that are game changers. We sharpened our focus. Ours was a single future state described in two words: gold only (i.e., more gold). That focus empowered us to achieve. Finally, our priorities were clear to all, inspired by His Highness's two words.

Distilling Direction in One Word

Some would be surprised that we are not referring to the usual mantras of developing "vision" and "mission" that are presented by all consultants. I don't see that it's functional or beneficial—and to each their own.

The direction does not need many words to present a crystal clear and unifying future state. I am sure that many examples will come to mind. Not only can direction be distilled into a sentence or even a phrase like "gold only." When it's really thought through well, it can even be one word.

Take a long, admiring look at the Emirate of Dubai and decipher their direction. This example is awe-inspiring. If one were to apply Modern Alchemy's premise to Dubai, it would seem that they have one incredible Due North, one guiding star that sets the emirate's direction. In my opinion, it's one word: destination.

In translating this direction, each of the directors, ministers, and managers, in their own realm of influence, would do their part to direct the ship toward that Due North of "destination." All want the world to aspire to come to Dubai. One would assume that the minister of tourism wants Dubai to be a tourist destination; the minister of education wants it to be an education destination; the head of banking wants it to be the banking destination, and so forth.

Now, how each of these individuals or departments does that depends on the individual decision-maker's sector-specific vision, provided that it fits into the overarching "destination" direction.

Does the word "destination" tell us what the city-state will look like in the future? No, but it tells us what direction it's heading in. And all Dubai ministers' instructions to their subordinates should be simple: "Get us to the destination."

This is the Due North approach. And when you are evaluating your direction, the actions that you require, the actions taken to date, and the individual performance, the questions become simple:

- Are we getting more or less of what we want? (In the case of the Dubai example, are we getting more footfall as a destination? And in the case of the Bahrain sport example, are we getting more gold?) The answer must be a binary yes or no.
- Are we heading toward the expressed future state we desire? Again, this must be a yes or no.

Focusing on and adjusting direction makes it obvious whether or not your future desired state is being achieved. It makes it measurable and attainable, not by setting goals but by comparing the delta or the difference between the past and the current.

Instead of setting goals, you cut through deceitful internal reports and statistics and the wishful thinking in forecasts. With this approach, everyone in your organization knows if they're doing a good job or not and everyone strives for the organization's success. It very quickly becomes blatantly clear to all if the organization is headed in the right direction. It becomes obvious for all to see. That's the advantage.

Getting Comfortable with Chaos and the Unknown

Have you ever paid close attention to how a butterfly flies, how it gets from A to B? It flutters around the flower until it reaches its target. One wonders whether there is even a target in the first place. Does a butterfly simply land in the vicinity of pollen-filled flowers and make the most of wherever the elements take her?

I fully appreciate and understand that the butterfly took off from a particular place, one presumes with the intention of having its future state be better than its old location or current state. It's that drive, I assume, that made it act in the first place. But I doubt that on a breezy day, it would have known exactly where it was going and exactly where it was going to land, let alone whether there would be pollen there or not.

It seems that life or business is more of that chaotic fluttering and much less a planned straight route to success or completion. That's reality for you. And those that can embrace such chaos or unknowns have over time, historically, made the most impressive strides and created the most impactful, world-changing platforms, products, solutions, and organizations.

A lot of individuals that I discuss Modern Alchemy with, particularly the Due North principle, assume that this is a project management exercise or tool. It's not. The reason it's not is that project management requires a finite, specific, time-based goal—with a start, milestones, and end—and a well-drawn-out plan setting out a route prior to launch and documenting all the risks along the way.

The amount of information required to put such a plan together prior to launch is daunting in real life when most variables are unknown; when dependencies are unknown; when resources are not guaranteed; when individual players and stakeholders are unpredictable, unreliable, and readily influenced. Such a position, from a project management perspective, is paralyzing, to say the least. No great initiative would ever get approval if it relied upon a standard project management approach.

Modern Alchemy is meant to break you out of that mental prison. It focuses not on reaching arbitrary milestones but on defining one's direction. The difference here is that with a direction, a Due North, one keeps moving north even when things go wrong, even when the unpredictable occurs. The point isn't to reach the Due North, because there's nothing to reach. Rather, the point is to go through the infinite course of iterative development with limited information and a flexible mindset that isn't dependent on external milestone-based validation, knowing fully well that there is no actual destination and yet not allowing the lack of destination to impact the group's drive nor productivity.

The fact that most companies or organizations adopt the old, legacy, finite project management approach is probably why most organizations and individuals do not take leaps or make ripples. It's probably why their innovation is limited. It is for this reason that one should get comfortable with the unknown and chaotic nature of reality, relying on very simple elements and steps in playing this long and infinite game.

First, a group is to fully understand its current state and the reality of its position with all its intricacies. This is essential. The reality of the situation must be faced and assessed with all its nuances.

Second, a group is required to know and commit to its direction, which must be communicated with all its elements clearly.

Third, the group must recognize whether the current state is better and closer to Due North than if it were to act or move. If not, and if acting or moving gets the group's alignment closer to Due North, then the organization or the department makes the iterative change.

This process continues indefinitely.

The Weakness of Future Authoring

This realization that unknowns are a fact of life and a part of reality puts Modern Alchemy at odds with a popular self-discovery exercise pushed by personal development authors in recent years called "future authoring." Their idea is as follows: You write the script of where you want to be in the future, plot point by plot point, turn by turn, twist by twist. You would write this all out in detail down to listing the ages, even the dates, when you would achieve these milestones. (For example, by age thirty I want to make this much, by age forty I want to own this property, by age fifty I want to have a doctorate, and so on.) The idea here is to give the author milestones and targets and motivate them to improve themselves by giving them something to aspire to. The intent behind it is good, as it is meant to get unmotivated groups to work toward the things they want.

On the surface, future authoring has a lot going for it. Many teams are unmotivated and don't know what they want, and future authoring provides them with focus. Many of them have dreams of great success and want a push to get them there, so they make promises to themselves about what they will do. It encourages talent to see themselves as the type of person who can succeed.

However, it has a problem: The world doesn't conform to your plans, and there is no way to anticipate every possible change or eventuality. Future authoring is structured a lot like career planning and has the same fundamental problems: It lays out specific milestones that you're supposed to reach in exchange for some kind of benefit. It structures things as a chain of events leading up to a goal. A lot of future authoring plans are about completing specific tasks and receiving external approvals.

The truth is that this approach sets up groups to fail. The reality of the matter is that the random and chaotic nature of life is a fact that is much more reliable than the assumptions in the plans required for future authoring. As opposed to business school case studies, there is no fixed structure; things can happen for an infinite list of reasons. Doing the work and investing the effort does not guarantee a good outcome.

What happens when the business you always planned to acquire shuts down? The milestone would be impossible to meet although the effort is made and resources allocated. What happens when the demand you were planning to supply and the customers you were planning to serve are no longer interested or available? What happens when a recession makes it difficult to get those talents? What happens when a global pandemic shuts down supply chains that you need as part of your milestones? Even if you wrote those possibilities into your script, something else will eventually happen that derails your plans. It's a fact and eventuality that the group must embrace: that things will not effortlessly go your way.

There's also the idea that the plans themselves are unworkable. For example, you may want to secure a particular approval, but getting an approval depends not on your ability but on whether the officials or decision-makers will accept your application. These factors are outside of your control. You are at the mercy of chance, and the sooner this gets configured into your assumptions and your overall algorithm, the better it is for the group.

Despite its good intentions, future authoring and documenting business or organization strategies in such a manner is not a productive way to build that future. If anything, it eventually kills any residue of motivation within the team because of the daily setbacks that are eventual because of the rigidity of the undertaken process.

Milestones will be missed daily. This will zap whatever momentum you seem to be building as a group, and these zaps will come in daily considering the randomized nature of reality. The sooner this reality is recognized, the better it is for all.

Learning from the Military

Getting comfortable with unknowns and still being successful is not impossible. Just think of the military, which I have come to respect tremendously. They have a famous phrase: "No battle plan survives first contact with the enemy."

Think about that for a second. This simply means that the way you plan needs to be fluid. Everything changes, and you should expect and prepare for the unexpected.

Modern militaries follow a process known as "backward planning." They imagine a desired future state, figure out how to get there before the battle commences, and continue to iterate the plans during combat depending on the information that is coming in. It lets them stay fluid to account for the unexpected variables that always come up.

As long as the desired future state is clearly pictured, they are more flexible when modifying the specific steps they take in approaching it.

Think about it. A commander on the field has limited access to superiors at the base, but the team is aware that the plan is to take a castle. Whether one digs a tunnel or breaches the boundary walls, whether they parachute in or encircle the fortress, all listed options provide the same outcome. The commander is free to decide the details within the parameters based on the visibility and information he has. This fluidity and flexibility build into it the chaotic nature of reality.

The idea is best understood when compared to more rigid examples. Think of rigid command versus guerilla warfare. To illustrate the dangers of rigid, milestone-oriented thinking, let's consider the famous example regarding US involvement and engagement in Vietnam. The US approached that war with a seemingly short-term mindset; the plan was to face North Vietnamese forces head-on, overtake their forces in head-to-head combat, declare victory (which seemed inevitable considering the difference in strength and capability), and go home to a parade. That was the plan.

However, it didn't turn out that way. Although US troops held the battlefield advantage over their Vietnamese adversaries, the Vietnamese played the long game. More importantly, they played the *mind* game and frustrated all American efforts to get the forces to battle directly. The Vietnamese exploited weaknesses in American supply chains. They exploited the nature of the forest battlefield. They exploited the Americans' impatience and need for a quick victory. From a battlefield perspective, there was no question that the American plan simply did not work.

With all that, one thing is for sure: Military personnel have reached a supernatural level of comfort when it comes to dealing with unknowns and the eventuality of dealing with the unexpected. There is a lot to learn from them—and I believe that adopting a direction-based Due North approach brings one closer to the military-like focus on identifying opportunities to move forward.

Adopting the Infinite "Do" Approach

Think of the Japanese martial arts—aikido, judo, and even karate, which in Japan is called karate-do. That *do* at the end means "way"—not just a method but a physical path, almost a state of mind of continuous development. Any real martial artist would tell you that learning, experimenting, and training never end. There is no fixed target that you are trying to achieve. You are going for continuous refinement.

The martial arts don't represent physical pathways, nor do they represent individual milestones. Instead, they are something you have to practice continuously to sharpen a skill and stay sharp over time. It can be symbolized by a road that never ends. If you wish to travel down this road, you cannot stop. There is no end goal, only the journey that continues indefinitely.

For the exact opposite method found in the same field, one may look at the colored belt system which was adopted and localized for Western consumption. This is the exact opposite of the "do" approach. Here's how it goes: You start with a white belt. You memorize one choreography, get tested, and get awarded a colored belt. One proceeds to progress through the colors (some variation of yellow, red, green, blue, etc.) until reaching the black belt, meant to signify a static point of expertise, a fixed destination at the apex of the martial art journey. The idea is that the black belt marks the end of your training. Once you have it, you are done.

This goes against the whole idea of "do," where you are never done.

Now Japan is not immune to this fixed static mindset; they have a similar system of kyu and dan ranks for martial arts which sometimes takes on too much prominence, diluting the focus on the reason behind undertaking the martial art in the first place.

The original point of the martial art, I assume, was not the ranking system. On its own, it's a good motivator when viewed on a microscale, similar to dopamine triggers or likes on social media. But in the grand scheme of things, these micro dopamine doses don't help much if they're released at fixed intervals instead of naturally being released when participants or groups reach new levels or refinement or achievement.

If you had a Due North of "become effective at fighting," imagine how the whole ranking system would be different. Imagine how the practices would be different. Everything would flow toward refining your fighting abilities.

I would argue that breaking martial arts into *katas*—very exact and rigid scripted maneuvers—weakens the individual's ability to fight effectively, as opposed to strengthening the person. Needless to say, when confronted by an enemy, one can't demand that the enemy stand in a certain position or start with a punch, as is done when practicing the choreography.

The same concept applies to organizations. The direction should be clear; the route is discovered jointly on the way. The purpose is to get one degree closer to Due North.

The irony, of course, is that setting a course Due North also means you will never reach Due North. Obstacles on the way will always force one to maneuver around or over, which will always impact the direction, at times greatly and at times slightly. To paraphrase Cavafy's poem "Ithaca," it is the journey that matters, not the destination.

As a Modern Alchemist, you will continually evaluate your actions in terms of whether you're heading in the right direction depending on your adopted Due North. This may run counter to how you were trained. Because Due North is a direction instead of a destination, it may seem overwhelming. You not only have the freedom to reach that Due North however you please, but you also have room to navigate the inevitable setbacks. For all intents and purposes, even setbacks at that point are no longer recognized as setbacks; they are simply lessons that the group benefits from.

Just like the martial arts, Modern Alchemy is never-ending. You're not trying to reach or achieve anything fixed in time or place but continuously orienting yourself toward getting better at what you do.

Of course, this goes against everything that practitioners of setting S.M.A.R.T. goals and milestones believe in, and so the resistance to implementation within your group or organization might be high. But one need only point to successful examples of using non-S.M.A.R.T. goals—such as the efforts by Charles Koch, for example—to start to melt away such resistance.

For reference and example, Charles Koch explains his methods and his philosophy beautifully in his book *Good Profits*, which sets out his performance- and alignment-driven philosophy based on first principles. He shows how a company can operate and grow to great heights without budgets and the usual corporate S.M.A.R.T. tools.

The problem with S.M.A.R.T. goals is that they are either over-ambitious or under-ambitious. They're almost never just right. Let's say a group has already exceeded expectations in the first quarter. They stop or slow down. And by the next year, when the new goals come in, they have to rev up again, which is idiotic because so much time and effort has been wasted.

If the S.M.A.R.T. goals are not met, it's worse, because then you're teaching the organization it's okay to not meet goals. That creates an adverse culture of low standards and passivity when it comes to losing a challenge. One should never allow his people or team to be okay with losing.

S.M.A.R.T. goals *can* work, but only if there is serious accountability for not reaching them. That means firing people, which creates a terribly harsh work environment. S.M.A.R.T. goals push organizations to hire people and work them until burnout, which is terrible for staff retention and terrible for morale, instead of giving them a direction and allowing them to compete internally to show off their abilities.

There's no question in my mind that Due North—like the Japanese "do" with its continuous cycle of innovation and improvement and iterative, opportunistic, gradual steps in the intended direction—is infinitely more suited to reality and infinitely more productive in the long term that attempts to predict all variables and set rigid goals.

Following Due North

Once one has the direction set and once one is clear about the values (namely the red lines that one is not willing to cross), the rest of the exercise tends to fall into place.

This level of clarity comes into play in recruitment, in customer acquisition, in the provision of products and services, in almost everything that is adopted by any given organization.

Such clarity, once reached, allows you to have parameters for all your answers. When communicated with your talents, it allows you to scale and delegate the decision-making process without much resistance and without undue challenges.

The next steps are to find the people and talents to help you on your journey, to identify their parameters, and finally provide them with instructions on what to do more of and what to do less of during your ongoing iterative journey.

Audit Your Direction

1. Is your organization heading toward a future state that's desired by everyone in the company? Yes ☐ No ☐

2. Have you identified the people in your organization who do not want to head toward that future state? Yes ☐ No ☐

3. Can you describe the difference between an organization's (finite) objective and its (infinite) direction? Yes ☐ No ☐

4. Can you clearly write out the Due North for your organization? Yes ☐ No ☐

5. Does your Due North have a binary yes/no outcome to evaluate whether or not it was met? Yes ☐ No ☐

6. Do you know your values, namely the things you will not do to get to your Due North? Yes ☐ No ☐

CHAPTER 4

THE ALIGNMENT

On the 23rd of January 2018, the corporate world and, more importantly, the shareholders of Tesla woke up to some interesting news. There had been significant concern over recent years on the future prospects of Tesla as a company, and rumors were rampant about Elon Musk's impending departure from Tesla to focus on bigger projects, namely, interplanetary transportation.

News of the deal was covered by all the leading newspapers, including *The New York Times*[2] and *The Guardian*[3]. The consensus was that the deal negotiated by the Tesla board of directors was a huge coupe for Tesla and its shareholders. The premise was simple: Tesla had a market capitalization of around $50 billion at the time; if Elon was able to increase the market capitalization to $650 billion within a ten-year period, he would get a payment of

---

[2] Andrew Ross Sorkin, "Tesla's Elon Musk May Have Boldest Pay Plan in Corporate History," *New York Times*, Jan. 23, 2018, https://www.nytimes.com/2018/01/23/business/dealbook/tesla-elon-musk-pay.

[3] Rupert Neate, "Elon Musk lines up $55bn payday – the world's biggest bonus," *Guardian*, Jan. 23, 2018, https://www.theguardian.com/technology/2018/jan/23/elon-musk-aiming-for-worlds-biggest-bonus-40bn.

$55.8 billion. If he failed, he would get nothing. It was binary, all or nothing, with no provisions for salary, no cash bonuses, and no equity that vests with the passage of time. The deal required that Elon Musk stay in the role of CEO for a period of ten years, thereby alleviating any shareholder concerns about executive keyman risks.

The newspapers and the analysts were clear that this was the best alignment of executive and shareholder interests that they'd seen. The chairman of Tesla's compensation committee said it best: "It's heads you win, tails you don't lose," meaning if Mr. Musk was gaining billions, then shareholders were winning too. And if Mr. Musk did not perform, shareholders paid nothing.

Fast forward four years to 21 April 2022. People woke up to *The Guardian*'s news, which read, "Elon Musk poised to collect $23bn bonus as Tesla beats targets."[4] The seemingly impossible task was reached. Elon Musk had turned Tesla into a trillion-dollar company. Along the way, they made the shareholders and the employees untold millions.

What about the reaction from the stakeholders and some shareholders? Julia Davies, a member of Patriotic Millionaires UK, a group of super-rich people campaigning for a more equal society, presented the sentiments best when she commented that this was a perfect answer to the question, "When does a person have too much money?"

Needless to say, by 14 November 2022, after having achieved the miraculous goal and secured the future of the company, Tesla

---

[4] Rupert Neate, "Elon Musk poised to collect $23bn bonus as Tesla beats targets," *Guardian*, April 21, 2022, https://www.theguardian.com/business/2022/apr/21/elon-musk-stands-to-collect-23bn-bonus-as-tesla-surges-ahead.

found itself in court trying to defend itself and the package it offered to Elon. No one was claiming that the seemingly impossible was not an achievement; they were simply claiming that the numerical sum of the compensation is "too much" for someone to receive, regardless of the gamble or the achievement.

I have yet to come across a better example of alignment and an even better example of what not to do when achievements are reached and when it's time to honor deals.

Remuneration

When the organization wins, everyone wins. When the organization loses, everyone loses.

This is the essence of Modern Alchemy's focus on aligning the interests of the individual partners and employees with the organization. By aligning individual benefits with the intended outcomes of the organization or the project, and individual compensation to individual performance, everyone has real skin in the game and focuses on delivery. This gives them an incentive to go the extra mile and automatically penalizes them for falling behind.

When interests are aligned, alchemy occurs organically from the bottom up. We have a lovely Arabic quote that best encompasses this spirit: "May the spoils [of battle] be distributed." From experience, I've noticed that true superstars and high achievers will not join the march and will not continue to add value if the spoils are not justly distributed, in line with the original agreement.

What's more, the simplest way to stall any form of progress and give reason for an internal, eventual exodus of talent is by simply reneging on the deal to "distribute the spoils."

Swimming Lessons for Kids

Distributing the spoils is an interesting concept. It's a bit theatrical, but does it work with all sorts of projects, big and small, or is this an organizational change tool? The answer is simple.

Let me give you a very simple, personal example to confirm the proposition. I have two sons. I wanted the first son to learn how to swim; we were worried about them playing around a pool without knowing how to swim. This was important to us, and we were not going to cut corners when it came to costs.

He did about ten months of classes, three times a week, with a seemingly reputable teacher and organization. I distinctly remember that whenever I asked about the child, I remember he was either coming or going to swimming classes. I felt like I was living with an Olympian.

Then one day, we were on a family trip. He and I were standing by the edge of a shallow pool. I jokingly nudged him into the pool; he was already wearing his swimming attire anyway. He went in and hit the bottom.

He jumped up laughing, but I was freaking out. Why did he have to tiptoe in the pool? It turned out that he still couldn't swim alone without holding on to a ledge. You can imagine how disappointed I was. We had spent ten months taking him to classes, supposedly teaching him to swim, and this was the result? A "swimmer" who sank to the bottom of the pool and needed to tiptoe?

When we got back home from holiday, my wife sat down with our second child's swimming teacher and discussed our older child's outcome. She told him clearly that we didn't want an Olympian. We wanted him to be able to swim from one end of the pool to the other and back, just enough to make sure that he would not drown if he ended up in a pool accidentally.

The approach was simple: "This is what we're looking for. I want my son to be able to swim and swimming to the end and back is the binary test. How much do you charge, and what's the maximum you think it will take to get this kid swimming?"

He said, "Ten classes maximum."

"Fine, if it takes ten classes, how much would that cost?"

He gave us the price, and she said, "I'll give you this total, and then some. But I don't want it to be a function of time or classes. Show me my kid swimming, and then you'll get your money."

Like magic, instead of taking weeks of lessons as was the case with my other son, this one was ready in ten days. That's when my wife came home and said to me, "The swimming coach wants his money."

"There's no way!" I said. "How could he pick up swimming in ten days?" But my son had done it. Mind you, he was not an Olympian, but he could swim from one end to the other.

Why did my first son take months? Because the incentive structure was flawed. It was effort-based. No Due North was defined.

In the second case, I defined the teacher's Due North, and he could easily gauge whether he was getting closer to it or not. And it took him days instead of months.

We got what we wanted and the swimming teacher got what he wanted. We handed over his portion of the "spoils."

I appreciate how simple and intuitive it is when one presents the concept through this example.

These simple personal experiences from the lives of my children showed the absurdity of paying for time. Now, take a second to imagine how many interactions you have and how many service providers you currently remunerate based on time and effort as opposed to outcome—and imagine the potential if that were fixed.

How to Align Individual Benefits with Organizational Results

In this chapter, we'll discuss how to link individual decisions and performance to the proportionate gain to the organization. If an employee cuts costs or increases revenue (or both) they should receive a percentage of the organization's gains. This incentivizes employees at all levels to drive the organization to success.

Consider the ubiquitous McDonald's franchise. A supervisor may save incredible sums for the franchisee or franchisor by cutting unnecessary steps and speeding up processes. But if the supervisor doesn't receive any of those financial benefits, then why should supervisors make recommendations that would benefit the organization as a whole? Without this motivation, they generally don't, and potential benefits are lost.

The same goes for government employees. People rarely make recommendations to cut procedures that don't impact their compensation. They have no incentive to improve these procedures. It's better to keep their head down and do their busy work.

I can't emphasize how important this is: When you add incentives for positive change, it transforms everything.

One of my organizations worked with a Chinese founder who once told me, "Never underestimate the impact of even the tiniest award. It's not only that people are driven by financial incentive; it's also the dopamine hit which comes with achievement, even at the smallest scale." His entire company works from the premise that people are dopamine-sensitive and award-conscious internally and externally. Just a few cents (or pence or whatever your currency is) goes a long way. Don't pinch pennies. Reward your service provider and they will deliver to you better work that is many times more valuable than what you spent on them.

So it's not about how great the reward is. It's that there's an incentive to help the organization win more, win sooner, and win bigger. This works through financial rewards and also works with the dopamine rush that comes from being recognized for excellent performance, which spurs employees to do their best.

This concept can work for any service and any sector. Consider human resources as an example. An HR manager is there to bring the best talent into the organization. So track the manager's performance based on their new hire's performance. Giving the manager a financial incentive for hiring star employees gives them an automatic deterrent for hiring a dud. Losing their job is the ultimate disincentive.

Pick the direction you want the employee to go toward. Then let the employee know the direction, their responsibilities, and their metrics. This way, you make sure you're investing your talent's time in worthwhile matters. That's how you align individual and organizational interests.

I appreciate that some would argue that placing such clarity allows employees and service providers to "game" the system. Honestly, as long as they are getting the organization closer to the "end state" that is targeted, let them game all they want.

Oddly, this approach should be intuitive, yet most of the world doesn't follow it. Here's how to make incentivizing employees second nature.

How to Incentivize the Outcomes You're Paying For

Flip through 95 percent of job descriptions worldwide. You'll notice the retainer ends when success is achieved. Employees have no reason to achieve success in the first place. They are disincentivized from doing what employers want them to do.

It's bizarre, yet most organizations practice this misalignment. It doesn't have to be this way.

An Extreme: Chinese Emperors

I have heard an exaggerated and extreme example, but it's one that aligns interests. It's said that when some old, ancient Chinese emperors died, their servants were buried with them to serve them in the next world.

The simplest way to stay alive, then, is to protect the emperor and keep him alive as long as possible. It couldn't be simpler. Disturbing, but aligned.

Medical Professionals: General Practitioners

In the United Kingdom, every family tends to have a retained general practitioner (GP). GPs are paid whether or not a family sees them. Instead, the GPs are incentivized to keep family members alive, well, and healthy, so GPs collect and analyze the family members' health information and berate them if they do anything unhealthy.

Think about it. If a family member gets sick, a GP has more work to do but doesn't earn a higher rate, seeing that the fixed retainer does not change. If the family members die, the GP stops getting paid his retainer. So the GP is incentivized to keep you alive and healthy with no need for medical treatment.

Cleaners

Now imagine a bookstore that hires cleaners to dust the shelves every day. But the cleaners always leave the windows open, which lets more dust in. The store needs to incentivize the cleaners to close the windows.

If they were paid a monthly retainer based on time and effort regardless of how clean the store was, they would simply go through the motions. If it were outcome-based, they would work smarter, not harder, because working fewer hours would earn them more per hour relative to their retainer. This would encourage them to take steps, like closing the windows, to make their job easier. They would benefit and the store would benefit.

Back to First Principles

One must try not to forget that the true objective of compensation is to reward staff for accomplishing tasks or responsibilities, not to reward them for the time and effort invested in the task.

Remember the swimming coach example from earlier in the book? A coach's role is to impart or improve a skill, so the coach's pay must be performance-based. But coaches cannot be the ones who assess performance. Students and teachers must be in the same boat.

Once you grasp this principle, it's impossible to think about performance and incentives any other way.

Examples of Misalignment

Once you see the impact of "pay for performance" as opposed to "pay for effort," it's very difficult to unsee it. I will share with you a few examples which I am sure will trigger your mind to throw up an endless array of examples that you always knew and felt weren't right.

Let's start with oncology. Think about it for a second. For as long as the patient is sick, and every time a cancer patient comes in to receive chemotherapy, the chemo center gets paid, the oncologist gets paid, and the pharmaceutical company gets paid. Every level in the chain will stop reaping the benefits if the patient beats the cancer. It's a perverse incentive structure if you really think about it, honestly.

Imagine you're driving down the street smoking a cigarette. Your doctor is next to you. Will he make a big fuss about the fact that you're smoking? If his interests are aligned with yours, of course he will.

Fitness trainers worldwide discuss weight loss and muscle gain. But they are incentivized and remunerated based on time. How does that make sense? Why not link the two? That way, they earn money only if you lose weight, not if you just show up.

Once you understand the performance and incentive structures, you can identify superior alternatives with better-aligned incentives. It's no longer a matter of effort; it's a matter of results.

Across all industries, a large percentage of people would not be able to deliver if their pay were purely tied to results. So it may not be practical in society-wide application, but you and your organization can still reap the benefits of incentivization.

Koch Industries implemented a compensation policy based on results rather than time and effort. Their oil tanker drivers were barred from changing vehicles for the length of their employment. As a result, management could tell if drivers took care of their tankers so as to require minimal maintenance. They added an annual bonus for drivers whose vehicles needed zero maintenance.

Just by aligning interests this way and doing so over and over again, Koch Industries transformed a $30 million company into a $50 billion company.

One objection to the Modern Alchemy method claims it's not fair to put so much pressure on the bottom of organizations, especially on employees who do more work for less pay. The problem is that line of thinking links effort to pay.

Modern Alchemy links pay to performance and risk. To increase your pay, increase your performance or your risk appetite. The more you invest, the more you get back. Apply that model to your company so anyone can get a pay raise by accepting more risk. It's like gambling when the odds are stacked in your favor. The more you wager, the more you get back in the event you win.

Go through your whole organization, department by department, to ensure the incentive structure is driving employees' work and focus toward the outcomes you want. Then design individual career paths for employees by playing to their strengths, clarify the deliverables required and the Due North, and ensure that compensation is readily made when milestones are met. That's the easiest way to ensure they get what they want at the same time that they are taking the company where it needs to go.

How do you structure your company to incentivize the outcomes you want? A reliable method is to structure reporting lines based on time preference and reflect the same in employment arrangements. We'll explore that tactic in the next section.

Finite versus Infinite Employment

In any business or organization, we use a very quick tool to visually identify where we can better align interests.

We believe that the owner and the shareholders have an infinite time horizon when considering their affiliation with the organization. It is true that the shareholders may sell their shares, but the incoming shareholders would then simply take their place with the same sort of alignment. Meanwhile, those below them—the board, managers, supervisors, etc.—have a finite time horizon.

Healthy Time Preference Chart

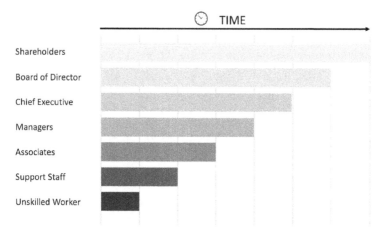

The lower you go in the food chain, the shorter the contracts should be. Managers are assessed every two years, supervisors every year, and so on. Down at the very bottom are unskilled staff who work by the hour.

In a misaligned organization, management and staff lower on the pay scale have more fixed durations of employment (i.e., longer contracts) than those who have more responsibility and compensation. Such an organization offers five-year contracts to management but only one-year contracts to board members. All the pressure is on the people at the top to execute because they only have one year, while the ones at the bottom are relaxed.

The tension for time and performance must be at the bottom. Only then does the top have enough time to be strategic in their thinking. If you ruin this symmetry, then the top has to play defense. Instead of looking for new opportunities, they're worried about the lack of buy-in, efficiency, or performance by their subordinates. As soon as they start playing defense, they're no longer playing to win—and you lose.

Unhealthy Time Preference Chart

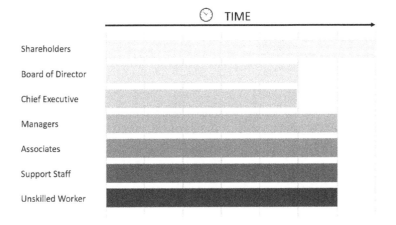

Consider family companies. Ownership is multigenerational. The executives have one-, two-, or three-year contracts, so the pressure is on them. Meanwhile, younger family members who work at the bottom of the organization have indefinite employment because they're presumptive future owners, which removes their incentive to perform and contribute to the company's overall success.

Unhealthy Family Company Time Preference Chart

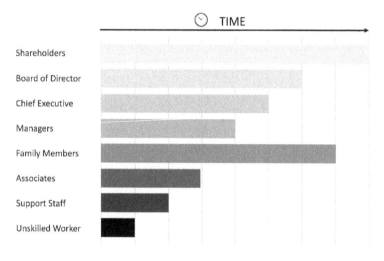

And the CEO can't fire subordinates who are members of the family. So turnover, when it happens, is forced to happen at the top among higher-paid, non-family members with more responsibilities. This creates a backward environment wherein the chief executive has to play defense instead of thinking strategically. The younger family members who are supposed to be handling the actual work aren't worried at all because their job permanence prevents them from reaching greatness.

You can see this misalignment in sports organizations too. The bottom waits for the top to fumble and leave. The head coach or manager has a one- or two-year contract, while older, often underperforming players are contracted for three or more years. The older players may assume they're irreplaceable, but the coaches are always on their tiptoes. And the coaches just can't move the underperformers. As a result, the team stagnates. For example, after winning his sixth NBA championship, Michael Jordan retired a second time from professional basketball. Then he unretired near the age of forty to play two seasons with the Washington Wizards. The team failed to post a winning season or reach the playoffs either year.

In a company with proper incentive alignment, the lower your paycheck and the lower your position in the organization, the shorter your guaranteed employment. Your job longevity is correlated with how much responsibility and risk you are willing to take on.

Anyone willing to receive minimal or no pay in exchange for equity or performance-based compensation needs to be at the top of the hierarchy, and those people should have the most decision-making responsibility. They should not be laborers who carry out line duties. The top of an organization is the choreographer, with the top performers right below. If you're at the top and running around like a headless chicken, something is wrong.

The only way you can prepare for changes in that imminent future is in a noise-free environment. That is not possible with day-to-day deadlines and demands always clamoring for attention. As Warren Buffett said, "I insist on a lot of time being spent, almost every day, to just sit and think. That is very uncommon in American business … I do more reading and thinking, and make less impulse decisions than most people in business." But he's absolutely right. This time to plan and think without interruption is essential.

Let's compare and contrast the White House with Buckingham Palace. The White House has daily fires to put out, drama to tweet about, and controversies to rope all staff into resolving.

By comparison, Buckingham Palace is like being in a library. Not even the sudden resignation of a prime minister can make the institution overreact and disrupt its program. You don't have to be a monarchical organization to appreciate a 1,200-year-old system and its priorities.

So, when applying this to business and leadership: When starting a company, you're trying to design a machine that can give the leadership the zen-like silence required to plan years ahead into the future and to analyze and assess risks. Design your hierarchy's time horizons so those lower in the organization can deal with the front-facing, day-to-day matters, which gives the managers room to develop strategies and tactics to capitalize on opportunities.

If you get this right, the top should not be tiptoeing, should be fully aligned to sink or swim with the organization, should have time to make informed decisions, and should be protected from day-to-day "drama."

But suppose your organization's time horizons are already misaligned. How do you correct them? Start with drawing out the contractual time preference for each of the layers, and then identify the glitches where a lower tier extends longer than the higher tier. Then, like combing long hair, start from the top and start rectifying one level at a time.

Audit Your Alignment

1. Have you built and communicated incentives for positive performance and not effort within your organization? Yes ☐ No ☐

2. Is your employment system built on a finite, performance-based model? Yes ☐ No ☐

3. Have your organization's contracts been modified to renew quickly for those with less authority, but respectively longer for renewal for positions with greater decision-making responsibilities? Yes ☐ No ☐

4. Are those in the top tier fully aligned commercially with the organization, sharing both its successes and its failures? Yes ☐ No ☐

CHAPTER 5

THE RESPONSIBILITIES

The Alchemist is selected.
The direction is set. The Due North is adopted.
The future is now clearer.
The most important question now is who does what.

Alchemists Never "Touch the Ball"

Before doing anything else, you have to remember that the Alchemist never, ever "touches the ball." The Alchemist "plays the orchestra" and never touches a musical instrument.

What does this mean in practical terms? It simply means that the Alchemist cannot shoulder an executive responsibility that will suck him into the day-to-day work.

Think of a sailing race example, which I think reflects this well. The skipper must always keep his eye on the direction the sailboat is heading or else the race will be lost. Look sideways, look back, and the race is statistically over.

Why is that, one may ask? When a skipper looks away, many things happen. The rudder is inevitably, if slightly, moved. The upcoming wave slams into the hulls, slowing down the vessel, instead of one surfing above the wave. The most efficient route is lost. You have to remember that life, like a sailing race, is never a straight line. You cannot have straight lines when there are waves, undercurrents, wind, and moving parts.

So, what is the skipper to do? The skipper has a full crew, each individually shouldering a number of responsibilities and each catering and serving a priority that is required for the Due North to be reached.

Picture the great Atlas with the world on his shoulders. We are all quiet Atlases in our own little way, shouldering what we can, what is beneficial for us to shoulder and what we believe we are duty-bound to shoulder.

What you want is an Atlas. What you're looking for is someone strong, reliable, predictable, and committed who can quietly and calmly shoulder responsibilities and take full accountability for them in return for a share in the overall group spoils.

In this chapter, we will explain responsibilities, the real building blocks of the organization. But first, a few words of caution.

Beware of Fast-Talking, Slick Sound Bite Peddlers

A book I read recently called *Noise* advises readers to find an Alchemist and simply close the door to any sort of layman's input. By doing this, you cut out 90 percent of the noise in your organization. The reason the majority of organizations fail is because they make the mistake of listening to individuals who don't know the details. It's like going on Twitter and asking your followers to vote on whether or not you should have surgery. There's no way your followers could know enough to give you helpful input. When you go to the masses and the masses aren't informed on the issue, it's only going to create a deluge of unhelpful information that gets dumped into your lap.

First, a crucial word of caution: Pick your shoulders carefully. You are going to be allocating responsibilities, so you need strong shoulders to place these responsibilities on, shoulders that are not slippery, shoulders that are straight and strong.

An Atlas is not loud. An Atlas is not a fast talker. An Atlas is not focused on external perception. He is focused on the weight being carried by his shoulders only.

Beware of sound bite peddlers. Beware of fast-talking, slick individuals who focus on external signaling. Beware of sacrificing logic for the attempted creation of a fog to blind the stakeholders. When the individual is "dancing" like birds-of-paradise, those spotlight-seeking birds with the intricate complicated dances that serve very little by way of purpose, remember to only assess them on the responsibility being shouldered and how that deliverable is being done. Do not get captured by the sirens of the sea whose beautiful performances entrance sailors and lead them to the rocks.

Remember always, you're never limited to only existing legacy talents. There is plenty of talent that can be organized and choreographed, even in the more rural of locations. But this only works if you set clear responsibilities and, from there, assess based on the performance of those responsibilities only—and not the added showmanship and the generated fog and noise of con men.

Responsibilities are worthless if they're not shouldered well.

Examples of Con Men

There is a particular experience that always brings a smile to my face and reminds me to be careful of falling into a simple trap.

At this critical junction in the organization's journey, one needs to focus on visualizing the conversion of the old current state to the future state. Sadly, this is also when investment bankers, consultants, and shamans usually make an appearance. They are usually very easy to identify if you're focused. These people tend to be loud and flashy; tend to evade deep, technical conversations like the plague; tend to drop and sprinkle names right, left, and center; tend to endlessly spew commoditized sound bites like "the adoption of KPIs [key performance indicators]," adopting "corporate governance models," copying "international best practices," and documenting "standard operating procedures," to name but a few; and they have no faith in logic or first principles.

Trust me when I say that these shoulderless sound bite peddlers will only waste resources and time and their supposed customized solutions.

This reminds me of a hilarious experience that I lived and witnessed firsthand years ago. An investment banker with a Santa Claus–like bag of new age investment banking sound bites and a perfect Western accent was engaged by a number of investors to start an investment bank. I was part of the team that was brought in to help make it happen. I'll never forget that first interaction.

I walked into a large conference room to see the Santa Claus character with his bag of sound bites at the head of the table. He had raised commitments from the investors to start the financial institution, and the regulators had granted the audience permission to take a deep dive into the business plan that this team was to present, having received their preliminary approval.

When asked what he needed to make this happen, he said he was working on the "golden" logo. He had decided to have his headquarters in a hotel because "all the best bankers have butlers," and the hotel could provide them with a butler. Then he opened his bag and dropped a few trending phrases during those days—"singularity," "Abrahamic finance," "Fourth Industrial Revolution," "quantum computing," et cetera—to the delight of the audience.

Needless to say, had someone slowed down the conversation to assess the link between the first sentence and the second, one would see that this was a cacophony of smart-sounding, recorded sound bites. It was like seeing a parrot in action, having lived in many households, having stitched together whatever his memory could recollect.

I loved it; I laughed for days. I immediately opted out of supporting the project—while laughing, of course. And if I'm to be honest, I'm still laughing today.

His recipe for creating a financial institution was (1) get a shiny logo; (2) get a boardroom or fancy meeting room; (3) get a butler; (4) sprinkle some new age sound bites. Do that and you're off.

As one expects, the fraud was eventually uncovered. Years later, after the bank was formed, my office got a call from some of the investors to assess the possibility of initiating legal proceedings to get their money back, an impossible task, seeing that their money was spent on conference rooms, butlers, logos, sound bites, and private jets.

From the outcome and the process he followed, I must assume he's not an Alchemist. An Alchemist would not have focused on the outward presentation, namely the logo, the butler, the sound bites, and the private jets. His focus would have been inward at this point.

Think about it for a second. How many people have you seen or heard skewing the most popular recent sound bites, only to see it all disappear—while, of course, the cons live it up in the meantime? Remember NFTs, fintech, blockchains, and recently, AI this and AI that?

These eloquent, slick cons are very easy to identify if you're paying attention and if you simply slow down the conversation to assess the words slowly. When in doubt, ask technical questions and watch them squirm.

My advice is to be aware of this risk, especially at this point in time in your journey from the current state to the future state.

In many situations, it's best not to waste time on allocating responsibilities to these types of individuals. All you will get is noise, and you will signal to the rest of the organization that you like and appreciate such noise-generating con men—which will risk everyone junior mutating into this form after seeing their seniors.

But if you must keep them, our responsibility protocols, which are to be explained in this chapter, will at least help.

Chairs or Roles and Not Individuals

Before addressing how our concept of "responsibilities" works, it is essential to note that an Alchemist never designs an organization around the existing talents only but instead must consider the talent pool available inside and outside the organization. This is essential if the organization is to compete properly and to scale.

Filling the Seats by Playing to Natural Strengths

The registry of responsibilities decouples the chair from the individual and separates the position from the person. What's the altered mindset that stems from this?

Most organizations operate from this premise, which I considered flawed: that the team members, the individuals, and the resources currently available in the organization are the only team members that will be available to fill these positions. That's absolutely incorrect.

If you want to create a truly open, competitive, and just environment, then it has to be open. It's quite literally the first prerequisite, and for the environment to be open, then you need to believe that both the potential talent outside your organization and the talent inside your organization should compete for these positions.

How should they compete? It's weighted, based on two elements. The first is the nature of the specialization itself, whether the person can plug and play, and whether they can deliver. The second bit is whether they were naturally destined or inclined for this sort of position based on their natural traits—God-given traits, for all intents and purposes. The result of this role assignment and reassignment is a crystal clear hierarchy and chain of command.

Consider as a great example what Bobby McFerrin presented at the World Science Festival on June 12, 2009, where he turned a crowd into an orchestra by simply delegating tasks and providing simple guidance.[5] It was a truly brilliant example of what guidance and collaboration can do. This was further developed by the likes of Jacob Collier in his shows, where he again takes an audience that has never performed together before and turns them

---

[5] Bobby McFerrin, "Bobby McFerrin Demonstrates the Power of the Pentatonic Scale," June 12, 2009, posted July 23, 2009, by World Science Festival, YouTube, https://www.youtube.com/watch?v=ne6tB2KiZuk.

into a finely tuned orchestra within a few minutes by simply seg-regating roles and choreographing.[6]

These assignments are based on specializations. Are the individuals you have naturally inclined to play a particular role? Is their character in line with the responsibilities of their position? In regards to the example above, high agreeableness, high extraversion, and being a "people person" aren't natural fits for an internal auditor, so find the role that's a good fit and put that person there instead.

This role assignment offers the benefits of specialization. If each individual is assigned a specific role, one suitable to his nature and skills, then performing those tasks he's responsible for comes without friction, rather than feeling forced to work. You'll get better results when people's talents are aligned with their responsibilities. It's that simple.

But to do this, you have to play to strengths and natural affinities. And this means *actual* strengths. Just because one member of your team's parents told him he was good at math doesn't mean he's *actually* good at math. There is a difference between a semi-firm grasp of Algebra 1 and knowledge of advanced calculus.

One group told us, "Our strength is we're good with people." But when we studied their personalities, we saw that the people they worked with were not eager to socialize with that particular group. In fact, we could tell from the reports that neuroticism was high in the group, while agreeableness was low. These were not individuals that were the life of any party, so to speak. "We're

---

[6] Jacob Collier, "Jacob Collier – The Audience Choir (Live at O2 Academy Brixton, London)," June 2022, posted August 3, 2022, by Jacob Collier, You-Tube, https://www.youtube.com/watch?v=3KsF309XpJo.

good with people" was a la-la land fairy tale their parents had told them, and that they still believed, despite data to the contrary. You have to assess talents by actual, measurable metrics, not just by what people say they are good at.

Most people in your organization probably haven't had the opportunity to define their strengths, so you may have to go back to basics to define these individual strengths and affinities for each person. Do what you need to do to get an accurate assessment. This is worth your time.

Now, once roles and responsibilities are delegated, there can be no micromanagement. The individuals have their responsibilities, and they will be expected to follow and meet them.

We can scientifically test for both traits and specializations. It just takes a bit of time. Now, as anybody in management knows, the skills and qualifications are easy to upskill (meaning to deliver certain skill sets to that child), to build or learn if they are absent or deficient, but it's the traits that are simply impossible to change.

When reassigning roles, do *not* try to change the natural state of individuals. If someone is not confrontational, don't try to make them confrontational or send them for training on how to be more confrontational. Make sure you know who they are and where their strengths lie and then play a creative game of musical chairs. Swap them for someone who *is* naturally confrontational and equip that person with the skills that they would require for that position.

In most organizations, they do the exact opposite of this when assigning people to roles. If they want a PR person, they would ask who has a PR background or specialization without checking whether their traits fit or don't fit a PR position. But if someone is in PR, you want that someone to have high conscientiousness and also have high extroversion. Without this, they can't do a good job at PR, no matter their other skills or experience.

I would much rather have someone in a position where their traits fit their position rather than someone who has the qualifications but whose traits just don't fit. No square pegs in a round hole.

For another example, I interacted with some youth as the minister of youth and sports. During my interactions, the youth centers were complaining about how bad a certain individual was. I had to explore the issue. Why was he bad?

Number one, this person stayed home all day; he was an introvert. He lived an isolated life with few people whom he felt understood him. Number two, he was unhealthy because he stayed home all day with little exercise and social stimulation.

The argument from a youth soccer scout and the regional youth centers was that this kid was not on a promising path to adulthood. There was nothing that could be done for this child, and they conjectured that he'd end up with some sort of drug problem. That was the reality of what I had to deal with.

This is what we did. We created a new program to focus on the positive elements of youth as opposed to the negative. We incentivized talent scouts (and parents, for that matter) to shed light on the young talent they knew of in the areas where they lived. We financially incentivized these centers through a grant system where the more young talent they found, the higher their weight with the grant distribution cycles. The idea was to play to their strengths.

And lo and behold, you can imagine where this went. One day, after we had changed the system and the method by which we distributed grants, I got a call saying that the local youth center adjacent to the problematic young person's residence wanted to meet with me. When they arrived, they were carrying a portfolio with a young talent's pictures in it.

Their faces were shining with pride. They wanted to tell me they were showing off their youth as the jurisdiction's only Olympic esports champion. They wanted us to create a program together to upskill him. I had no idea what that was, to be honest. I asked them what they meant by esports champion. Turns out, it was competitive video games.

"Yeah, you don't understand," they said. "This guy has the discipline that nobody has. He can sit in front of a game and hack away at it for ten to twelve hours straight, with no breaks. He can do this for days on end."

The *exact* same individual had been mentioned to me before, but he was shown now in a completely different light. Before, they could only see the child as a "bum" that couldn't do X, Y, or Z. Now, they were presenting him as a talent they've now identified. They were dealing with the exact same skill sets and tendencies, but all we did was clarify the responsibility and clarify the direction. They looked for what their youth was good at instead of lamenting all the things he wasn't good at. This is the key.

The responsibility shift for the organization was to identify talents and shed light on them, to provide them with opportunities, and nurture them toward their own kinds of excellence. And just by virtue of doing that, it transformed people who had been reporting all the flaws of individuals and made them into people who found, focused on, and celebrated the positive.

What's funny is that these individuals at the youth centers were always inclined to see the best in kids because they were working in that field. Now, instead of flagging the worst in children (as they'd been previously instructed to do), we financially incentivized them to see the best in them. The results were truly staggering.

Do Not Change People. Change the People.

The biggest shame and the biggest waste of effort and resources is when organizations try to change people, sometimes with force and other times with carrots. One thing is for sure: The statistical chances of success are minimal at best. That means that even if you do succeed, you will fail, considering the resources that have been burned in the silly attempt.

That is Alchemists never, ever try to change people. They deal with people as they are. They figure out their strengths and play to said strengths by moving them to a position where these natural traits and tendencies can be beneficial to the organization, without any need for amendments.

One of the most important things that the Alchemist must do is to understand the talents that he's working with, to observe their natural state. This is why psychometric testing comes in very handy.

When you know what the role is, you can identify what traits the role requires, and then you test the suitability and the natural fit of the candidate's natural traits to that role.

Example – Selecting Sports for Kids

Think of how the best countries in sports play to their kids' strengths. They start by analyzing the child's natural physique, character, traits, abilities, and interests, and then they play to those. The best do not take a child and mold them into a role;

they instead discover together the best role for them based on their reality.

For example, we see how the best child programs analyze height, stature, bone density, metabolism, resting heart rates, and other key factors. Based on said facts, they select the sports that are introduced to the child and select the role within the sport that said child would play. Big hands? Goalkeepers. Short and thin? Jockeys. Tall? Basketball players. Broad shouldered? Swimmers.

Selecting the right sport allows the child to have quick wins, which will only reinforce his interest in developing further. This is important because a person is more likely to stick with something if they get good results early.

Remember what comes first. The coach first writes down a wish list for the position, characteristics, traits, and physical specifications. Only then do they start scouting.

So, the check is to see if the child fits the defined role, the proverbial chair, within the sport and not if the role can be customized around the child.

Example – Wrong Candidate for Internal Auditor

As an example, let's look at one of the situations one of our teams dealt with over the years. In an organization that we were given to turn around, we were due to receive individual audit reports every quarter. In the first few months of the project, the team was *sure* there were plenty of wrong things being done and plenty of mistakes that indicated noncompliance, but when I looked at the reports, there wasn't any sign of that. How could that be?

It turned out that the individual put in charge of internal audits was the kindest, gentlest, and most agreeable person in the organization, which sounds great, but also meant that whenever he had to file a noncompliance report, he died a little inside. It broke his heart to report someone for not following standard operating procedures or regulatory requirements. So his solution was simply to not report them, which left me with empty audit references and no idea what was going on. This was ultimately going to hurt the company. Problems need to be addressed, and this kind and agreeable person was poorly suited to managing the internal audits.

On paper, he was an incredible candidate. He had all the grades, he had all the accreditation, and he had years and years of experience. But it turns out he didn't have the stomach for it.

So we switched him over to a front-facing, people-pleasing job. Then we asked our scouts to find within the organization the most narcissistic and confrontational individual they could find, and give him the internal auditor's job (or the job of supervising them). As soon as we did that, the machine started moving forward, and the internal audit did what it was supposed to do. The job didn't change, just the person doing it.

Getting an internal auditor that has high extroversion, an affinity for people, and a penchant for saying yes, and then wanting them to report on individuals, is not a natural fit. While you have to check for specialization, this example shows that, more importantly, you need to figure out whether the individual is naturally inclined to play that role.

Communicate the Role and How It Fits

Rarely do we see organizations that are good at defining the role of the individual, the responsibilities that one shoulders and how they fit into the other responsibilities that are being shouldered by colleagues to create the "orchestra effect" or the "flow effect" that everyone is looking for.

One of the greatest organizations that I have come across that is excellent in communicating needs institutionally, as opposed to relying on individual people's talents in communication, is the military. The military starts with the goal at hand and initiates a "backward planning" exercise to move back to the milestones needed to get to the intended goal or direction. The plan is then broken down into roles and responsibilities, which are distributed to the soldiers.

The greatest of all communication and apprehension exercises, similar to a visualization exercise, is the "combat estimate" or "seven questions" process, where each soldier is due to respond to the following questions in writing:

1. What is the situation and how does it affect me?
2. What have I been told to do and why?
3. What effects do I need to achieve, and what direction must I give to develop my plan?
4. Where can I best accomplish each action or effect?
5. What resources do I need to accomplish each action or effect?
6. When and where do these actions take place in relation to each other?
7. What control measures do I need to impose?

The simple exercise of going through the motions, responding to these questions, and taking the time to "RedTeam" your plans at the very least instills and enforces the awareness of what is expected and how it fits into the grand scheme of things.

What's more, all instructions are documented in a journal that is referred to as a tactical aide memoire, which is a brilliant collection of institutional execution planning tools that are worth reviewing for any civilian, regardless of which sector they are in.

Finally, the military has the "one-third, two-thirds rule," which requests leadership to spend one-third of their time planning and segregating the responsibility building blocks and two-thirds of their time communicating them to their teams and supporting the execution of these plans. The simple fact that this rule exists forces the planning, forces the segmentation of roles, forces the selection of shoulder and personnel, forces the communication between the parties, and finally, forces the assessment of the support and upskilling required, if any.

Building Blocks

The very first concept that one must get comfortable with is that the whole organization is built on and stands on individual units, like atoms, that collectively carry the organization and push it forward. The organization is nothing but a pyramid of building blocks. These unique, individual building blocks are called "responsibilities" in the Modern Alchemy lexicon.

Before the butlers, the conference rooms, the public sound bites, and the private jets, one must define, refine, and assign these building blocks, these "responsibilities," that need to be carried on the shoulders of able, stable, predictable, and empowered individuals.

It is crucial to remember that a responsibility, once assigned, may only be allocated to one person; it can never be shared. Only one individual may carry the proverbial load of one item or deliverable. Even if the actual execution requires a group, one person must be solely accountable for delivery.

To better understand this concept, there are three forms of responsibilities segregated into two types or groups that I'll set out for you:

Type A1. A responsibility "**to deliver**" something once or on a periodic basis

Type A2. A responsibility "**to decide**" something

Type B. A responsibility "**to supervise**" a delivery or a decision

Each Type A1 responsibility to deliver or Type A2 responsibility to decide must have a corresponding Type B responsibility to supervise. What this simply translates to is that someone dedicated must be supervising and liable for ensuring the performance of the ones delivering and deciding.

In legacy organizations, they would talk about job descriptions, which are very open to interpretation and therefore open for misinterpretation.

With Modern Alchemy, each talent has a bucket of responsibilities. Their pay is linked completely to the successful completion of said responsibilities. Their performance reviews are primarily linked to the binary (accomplished versus failed) assessment of whether responsibilities have been shouldered well and delivered.

A Register of Responsibilities to Organize the Orchestra

Creating a registry of responsibilities allows you to zoom out from day-to-day operations and ask, *What is the purpose of this position?* And then, from that, therefore, *What are the responsibilities of the individual that will fill that position?*

The registry allows you to revisit the reason for existence for every rung on the organizational ladder. Why is this a task someone is responsible for in the first place? Now, by "responsibility," I mean task responsibilities, supervisory responsibilities, and also authority. We will return to these types again shortly.

For now, understand that we are focused on the work to be done and not the person doing it. When we say roles and their responsibilities, we do not yet mean not individuals. Roles, not people. Not personnel but chairs, positions that need to act in particular ways when interacting with each other.

At this stage of Modern Alchemy, you must be convinced of the need for these positions in the first place. You need to identify the specialization or skill set required for the successful completion of that position. *Then* you need to find the individual within the organization, or outside the organization, that is the right fit for that chair. You then need to make sure the individual knows the direction that you're going and, just as importantly, you need to make sure that this person is aligned with the team's intended outcome. They need to have the same Due North and be aligned with the intended future state.

This is the opposite of taking a person in an existing role and changing their responsibilities to try to make them fit the company's Due North. It starts with the position and its responsibilities, then finds a person well-matched to it.

Besides unmerited attention to standard operating procedures, the next biggest problem I come across in transformations to reach the future state is people-first thinking. I've spoken about this before in this chapter, but this is worth reinforcing. Here's what I mean. Most professionals talk about the current individuals within an organization and where they fit instead of talking about what the organization itself needs. This is an attempt to force square pegs into round holes. Try to force the fit, and you get disaster.

The Registry of Responsibilities

Role	No.	Function	Type	Responsibility
Internal auditor	XYZ-P001-F—1-R001	Compliance	Responsibility	Solely responsible for conducting annual internal operational audit for all the departments
Internal auditor	XYZ-P001-F001-S001	Compliance	Supervisory	Supervises compliance with internal controls
Internal auditor	XYZ-P001-F001-A001	Compliance	Authority	Authorized to flag the non-compliance to the CEO directly.

This was mentioned above, but the registry of responsibilities contains three separate registers: the registry of responsibilities, the registry of supervisory responsibilities, and the registry of authority.

Responsibilities are the expectations that a role has. The task is done right by the right date. It has to be something you can't weasel your way out of. There can be no excuses, only a binary yes or no. And it has to have a visually identified milestone with third-party verification.

Supervisory responsibilities are all about who ensures that the responsibilities are done right by the right date. This is the person who needs to make sure nothing falls by the wayside.

The register of authority is all about who has the authority to do what. Certain elements would need to be delegated to certain individuals or roles so that they can make decisions pertaining to those elements.

If we look at the auditor example, then the auditor's responsibility would be to make sure that they flag any noncompliance with the rules and regulations of the organization or, for that matter, the statutory requirements that are currently in place. The responsibility would also clearly state what the time frame is for the report to be delivered. That way, the auditor can manage their own schedule and their own plate because they know what the expectations are.

But for every responsibility, there is a corresponding supervisory responsibility. Who is going to supervise this person to make sure that their tasks are being done properly? Who reviews the work of the auditor? This would be the person that simply needs to check off whether the internal audit reports were provided at the right time on the right date. The register of supervisory responsibility is extremely simple but too often overlooked.

In regards to the registry of authority, if you believe in deep work and the focus state of work, you'd appreciate this. For both large and small organizations, elements would need to be delegated so people can make decisions pertaining to their work.

For the auditor example, someone will need to decide the next steps that need to be taken in regard to the items that were flagged for the internal audit. Do they simply go to HR and get the noncompliant team members trained? Is it something more painful? Is it a criminal violation that needs to be reported? The registry of authority will show you at every junction who needs the authority to do what.

Example – Soccer Team

As a somewhat silly but clearly visible example of how these registers interact, let's look at soccer teams. The responsibility of the goalie is to keep the ball out of the net, if you will. That's it. That's all he does, and it's a binary goal. If the ball passes into the net, he fails his responsibility. If the ball doesn't pass through the net, then great job. He's saved the team, for all intents and purposes.

Then you have the defensive lineman. They're not supposed to attack or do any of that. All they're supposed to do, in case there is an attack on them, is get the ball from the other team and give it to the middle linemen. Again, binary. They either take control of the ball and pass it onto their teammates, or they don't.

The middle linemen are supposed to figure out who on their team is positioned well, and then deliver the ball to them. Like the last two, binary. They need to deliver the ball at the right place at the right height, so the strikers can strike.

Now, once you look at it like that, you can look at many teams and realize quickly that possession of the ball is high with regards to certain teams, but they're still losing. However, if you start to recognize the responsibility of each team member, it becomes easy for you to identify where they're falling short.

You then need to address whether this is a skill problem or an incentive problem. What the experts found with Bahrain's soccer team was that our possession numbers were excellent. They were much better than we expected.

On the Bahrain national team, our goalies were excellent, and the defense was also excellent because nothing was getting to the goalie. When we looked at our middle linemen, they were doing great as well. They were prepping the shots.

It turns out our shortcoming was that we had a problem with the conversion rate of passes to shots on goal. There was resistance from the strikers to simply take the hits and shoot. What we realized is that there seemed to be an old sort of institutional memory about shots on goal, where the individuals who shoot on goal and miss are made accountable for missing the shot. They didn't want the social stigma of missing that shot, so instead of taking it, they passed it. And the whole team was losing for it.

We had ended up with strikers who just kept passing the ball rather than going for goals. But once that analysis was made, the solution became easy. We had capable players, but all we needed to do was to make sure we incentivized them and provided them with the protection that they thought was necessary to ensure they weren't going to be penalized for attempted shots on the goal.

As soon as that was addressed, it was like magic. Bahrain's superstar strikers began taking shots for the goals and making those shots, leading the team to victory. This simple analysis made it possible for us to start reaping rewards.

The beauty of the registry of responsibilities is that it gives you an excellent way to identify exactly where the shortcomings are. If you can see them clearly, you can address them. And if responsibilities are extra clear, then accountability becomes extra clear. That way, you can quickly identify who did what and reward them for the good work they've done.

Organizing the Responsibility Building Blocks

If one were to visualize the building blocks in pyramid form, you would see the following:

a. A group of responsibilities collected into what we refer to as a "function"

b. A group of "functions" grouped together under a "priority"

c. The "priorities" grouped together under the organization's Due North

The way one should visualize it is as follows. If the organization were a pyramid, starting from the bottom, you would have the individual responsibilities. Groups of responsibilities would be referred to as functions, or delivery units. Groups of functions are grouped as priorities. At the tip of the pyramid would be the Due North that everyone is aiming for, a clear direction.

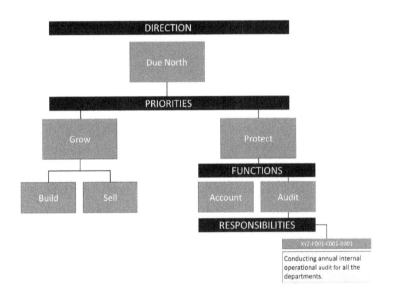

From Due North Into Priorities, Functions, and Responsibilities

To get anywhere, one must need focus, and for focus, one needs to remember what is important. So, the key is to know what matters most in your organization—and for yourself.

Remember that your company or organization is a going concern. Remember that a going concern cannot be all things to all people; priorities are essential. These priorities keep your eye on the long-term direction of the organization while reinforcing the focus on the Due North.

Since we met Due North a couple of chapters ago, let's remind ourselves briefly what this is and why it matters right now for Modern Alchemy.

For your company or organization to have a Due North, it takes much more than you deciding to make a change. The entire organizational structure of the company must be set up to point toward that Due North.

Underneath that Due North, you have your priorities. Think of priorities as the key elements that can help you reach your Due North. Each priority consists of functions that safeguard the priority; each function in turn has responsibilities attached to it. These responsibilities are the organization's lowest building blocks.

To carry out the functions, everyone has to perform their responsibilities. To follow the organization's Due North, the functions have to work as they should. The main job here is to leave out anything that doesn't get us facing Due North, because that creates problems for us.

However, every responsibility has a supervisory role attached to it, because someone has to make sure the work is done as planned. This supervisor calls out any shoddy work and corrects the employee who did it. This allows the employee to fix any mistakes so that on their next performance review, they get a better score.

The supervising party or Contractor has to keep the Associates in their orbit on track. Should they not do so, the functions will be harmed, then the priorities, and then the company will be taken away from its Due North and drift off track.

This is what happens in real life, more times than one can count. Too many organizations waste time on things that don't get them where they want to be. This is because they haven't defined their priorities. Instead, sidebar issues like office politics and problem employees take the lion's share of the organization's resources, instead of focusing on what matters.

Only when you define your priorities, which stem from your direction, can you really assess whether resources are being allocated efficiently. Organizations and individuals have limited resources, including limited demand, and one finds enormous demands on such time and resources. With clear priorities, clarity with respect to allocations becomes intuitive.

Hope Fund – Synthesizing Hope

Here's a real example of what I mean. I currently serve as chairman of a state-supported venture capital fund. We were sponsoring public projects and educational seminars. We were also buying stakes in small companies and attempting to upskill entrepreneurs. But there was a problem when we got started: We didn't have a Due North. We had an even bigger problem: Our deal flow was minimal at best, and our impact was not being felt.

These events were costing us money with no real direct returns that could be measured. I appreciated that we were "watering" the ecosystem—in line with the original proposal for the fund that the state's leadership had approved—but we wanted something much quicker, and we needed to be able to quantify success.

So, we slowed down and thought about it. In time, we found the direction we wanted: facilitate the creation of unicorns. We wanted the fund to support, invest in, and facilitate the creation of unicorn companies in Bahrain in any way. This did not necessarily mean that we (i.e., Hope Fund) had to own the unicorns. This meant that we had to activate the space, activate the entrepreneurs and their entrepreneurial spirit, activate the venture capital space, attract players into this ecosystem, and attract talents into the ecosystem.

The Due North was clear and the reason was clear. A unicorn company creates jobs and opportunities, brings capital into the country, and serves a vast number of key targets that the country wants and the youths need. And, needless to say, it succeeds in generating hope for other participants, therefore generating a positive outlook, which I believe is a self-fulfilling prophecy.

With a clear Due North, we could then set out our priorities, then our functions, and finally our individual responsibilities.

Our first priority was simply to invest in small, high-impact companies that could grow into unicorns. We therefore set up an investment arm to handle that matter, but we very quickly realized how difficult it is to identify opportunities without having a mature entrepreneurship and venture capital ecosystem. The work was tedious and difficult. We had to go to each company owner individually. That approach was not going to work.

We therefore realized that a second priority was to make noise—a lot of it. I am referring to the amount of noise we needed to attract and bring together key stakeholders in one place to have the investors, including our investment arm, meet the opportunities and the talents. The thought process was that this level of noise would bring the investors out, provided we could shed light on legitimately good opportunities that were vetted with strong due diligence having been undertaken. In the meantime, we could educate the masses about the opportunities, potential upside of entrepreneurship, and how investors are approached. This would help the ecosystem and would give the fund a better chance of reaching its Due North of helping create a Bahraini unicorn.

Our priorities were also set, and our department and functions reflected the grouping. Priority number one would be to create a team to identify opportunities and invest in them. This translated into the reaction of the investment vehicle and team. Priority number two would create a mechanism to shed light on the opportunities to allow for further opportunities to want to voluntarily approach us and other strategic value adding investors. This translated into the creation of a noisy, viral TV show that shed light on opportunities. Priority number three would be to create a mechanism to allow for the general public to co-invest in the opportunities. This translated into the creation of a crowdfunding platform.

How did we do?

We knew we were on the right track when our show was marked as the most popular regional show on Shahid, a regional streaming platform like Netflix. The show was called *Beban*, or doors, which stands for opportunities. The number of deals made (and are continuing to be made) on the show and outside the show far exceeded our expectations. We now have an active audience throughout the region with an active investor base and hoards of incoming opportunities. We're definitely on the right track.

In no time, the fund had raised funds from limited partners from the private sector, which brought incredible know-how and networks to the table. In no time as well, we had developed a media arm that produced a very popular local and regional TV show called *Beban*, which presented investment opportunities to SMEs to select groups of investors which was attached to a crowdfunding app that better presented current offerings to the public in one place.

One would ask (or one should ask, and rightly so), is this a media enterprise or a state-backed venture capital fund? To answer the question, we need to come back to the reason why the fund was incorporated in the first place.

Youngsters in the country were hearing about unicorns in the West but seeing nothing of the sort within the immediate vicinity of their worlds. There were a handful of stellar success stories that were seen in a few neighboring countries, but none of them resonated or connected.

And so, the fund was a communication and education vehicle first. It served a noble purpose with the support of public funding and strategic partners while making financial returns for all involved and advocating for our entrepreneurs in parallel.

How does this translate into our format? Simple. Our Due North was unicorns, related to local entrepreneurial opportunities and success. Our priorities were to first find the opportunities, then groom the opportunities, then present the opportunities in the most public manner and create bridges between the opportunities and the capital.

For this to work, we needed the Partners and Contractors to focus on each of the functional elements within the priorities, namely the scouting and filtration process, the grooming process, the production and presentation, and finally the transaction.

The key landmark for us was when the first investor, being a member of the public, saw an investment pitch on the show

Beban, assessed the opportunity, and decided to participate by co-investing on the crowdfunding platform.

The public was more engaged and more interested in small local enterprises and opportunities than before.

We were therefore one step closer to our Due North. Are they there? Did we reach it? The simple answer is no; it's not how the system works. Keeping your eyes on your Due North ensures that you're on your way.

Separating Assessment from Performance

In any organization, segregating the performance assessment and review function from the actual execution function is key to delivering the output that is required. It's intuitive.

Education – Playing to Strengths and Targeted Upskilling

When taking a look at the education sector, which was a project that the team and I had been engaged to do, we noticed that this fundamental principle was not incorporated. This had tremendous ripple effects, needless to say, in the wrong direction.

The accountability for any subpar academic performance by the students was unclear. Was it the teacher's fault, the curriculum creator's fault, a facilities problem, a social problem, or were the parents the cause? These were just some of the questions that were constantly asked simply because the ownership of the roles or block of responsibilities were unclear and the supervisory or assessment roles were also unclear.

A simple correction and refinement of said roles and responsibilities, including the priorities and functions, would create the necessary environment for some wonderful results.

"Your Kids" versus "Our Kids"

Another example we had was education reform. The key observation was that the educators had passed the ball—they had placed the burden of education back on the parents who have no formal education training or experience. This was clear when one heard the feedback during the parent-teacher conferences where the teachers would tell the parents, "Your kids are doing badly," and then move on to other matters during the day.

The "Your kids" phrase defined the problem for us. We were not clear previously with the educators on what their "purpose" was: upskilling the students to prepare them for employment and for productive lives.

Therefore, if the educators successfully upskilled the student (as confirmed by third-party assessors), the educator has succeeded. And if not, the educator (not only the student) had failed.

For that reason and as part of a new education strategy, we made "employability" our Due North. We wanted students to be more employable than they currently are. We wanted to ensure clarity pertaining to roles and responsibilities.

The premise was that once our direction was clear, the educators would have to work to redesign the curriculum and the overall distribution of responsibilities to ensure that these students could go on to bigger and better things.

For this job, the educator's first priority was understanding the current market and what future demand would look like, because the kids had to learn skills that people would pay them for. Relevance was key. Their second priority was taking this knowledge and breaking it down into modules that the kids could learn. Their third priority was making sure the kids were placed on the correct tracks for a given profession; after all, you need both the desire and the ability to succeed at something. Their fourth and final priority was to assess whether the students learned any new skills at all; this was not going to be some program where we passed the kids along.

Here is how it should be done, as set out in the new education strategy. When the kids come in, they have a curriculum designed and updated in partnership with industry. To pass, they have to go through a particular set of classes and engage in feedback loops through their engagement in internship and projects being undertaken for industrial players. This allows them to retain a lot of the information for the long term so that they can use it and, in parallel, develop their communication skills while expanding their network. We aim to do all this with the aim of employability, so the skills they learn get them jobs—things like finance, accounting, and reading, with less focus on handwriting, memorizing, regurgitating, and the like. One should actively try to strip away everything that doesn't get us to our Due North, so nonessential subjects like that fall by the wayside.

Finally, the performance assessment of the educator should be done by an external party and should solely be linked to whether the student in their care has successfully reached their potential and achieved the target or not. Educators should be educators and not part of the assessment machinery, considering the clear conflict in that case.

The premise is simple. If the student has been accepted into the care of the educator, it is then the educator's duty and responsibility to ensure that the student reaches the intended end state.

Simply clarifying our Due North has created tremendous change in focus, change in circumstance, and change in use of funds and prioritization, and has resulted in very quick results. The educators' eyes are now clearly on preparing the student for their professional life ahead.

Creating Cohesion

We would argue that the purpose of an Alchemist is to work to create cohesion between a high-impact and high-performance team or community of individuals. If you agree with that concept, then by virtue of that, the whole concept of asking supervisors to assess their underlings is completely wrong as set out in the previous section.

You should assess their underlings in the same exact way you do in a testing process: through an objective, independent third party that brings in binary reporting requirements. Did this person do X, yes or no? It should be straightforward and unbiased.

The more employees a supervisor has under them, the more authority they will have over individuals. By virtue of that, they are rewarded (or at least, not punished) for showing too much favor on low performance . . . until this new alignment is in place.

You're opening a can of worms just by asking managers and supervisors to assess performance. News of a negative assessment can come back to bite them, potentially turning their employees against them.

Sum of Parts Assessment

But by aligning performance, you create almost a brotherhood. In battle, you don't select the individuals who are with you, but you develop cohesion anyway. Why? If one person screws up, the rest fall as well, and you know that. The band of brothers forms by looking out for each other and developing a group identity.

The recommendation is for you to find ways of aligning outcomes for all employees to ensure a win-win, lose-lose outcome from the independent assessors, which can be set out in a method similar to that provided below.

Example – Aligned Schooling

Now imagine if, in schools, the teacher's income (and whether they continue in their job or not) depends on the academic outcome of the student he or she has. Imagine if the principal's outcome on whether they continue or not depends on the performance of the teachers under them! And imagine if all the testing was independently executed by an external source.

If that were the case, could you imagine how the system would change? There'd be a revolution in how teaching is done practically overnight!

Let's imagine this academic example with simplified numbers. Let's say you have a principal, who has ten teachers, who each have ten students. The performance of the principal is out of 100 percent, so that effectively means for every student who fails, he loses a percentage.

Let's say five students from the first class fail. The teacher by default gets a 50 percent score, but the principal still gets a 95 percent score, because it's five out of a hundred students. So the teacher fails because half of her students failed, but the principal is still passing; it's just 95 percent rather than a hundred.

The principal would either change the teacher or move around the students and figure out what they need in order to be able to cross the threshold. Say they identify that a child is dyslexic.; there are ways that kids with dyslexia can easily be supported in their academic journey.

Instead of a teacher telling parents, "I'm sorry, but your kid failed," she'd probably be doing everything she could to prevent those kids from failing.

With this, we can see the problem right now. The "sum of parts" method shows that everyone is responsible for the functioning of a department and that a mediocre effort in one place reflects on everyone. No finger-pointing can take place, and this emphasizes that change is a team effort.

This has a very beneficial effect: It forces a conversation about the department's performance. What usually happens is that the leader of the department doesn't wish to express shortcomings in the department, as that will reflect poorly. That manager has built up a lot of relationships in that department, and calling out poor performers sounds too much like calling out a friend. This manager then thinks that either change is not needed or that it can happen another time—and another time never comes.

But with a performance appraisal that considers everyone, there is no escape. A bad score reflects bad management, and the leader must own up to it. This forces the manager to make sure that all subordinates are putting forth their full efforts, achieving all objectives and milestones—and this applies to everyone in the department who has responsibility over someone. Because the whole department's reputation is affected, everyone has to achieve every objective set before them. And that means the manager must have that difficult conversation. The organization has a purpose, and that purpose must be fulfilled, with no room for excuses.

With direction, priorities, and functions crystal clear, we can now discuss the responsibilities—more specifically, how to track and assign them.

Failing Organization Structures

For one to understand the idea further, you have to consider and visualize the opposite to know what to do.

Take a proverbial organization. Whether private or public, you have a chief or leader who would in turn have a second-in-command, and, of course, a third-in-command.

Now, imagine if the parties were assessed independently. Imagine if the second-in-command can only be promoted if the leadership is removed. Imagine if the only way for a third-in-command to be a second-in-command is if that person leaves, is fired, or gets promoted.

When you take a step back and look at this organization, it's in everybody but the leadership's interest for the leader to be fired because everyone would move one step up. This is hilarious yet awful to think about. Imagine intentionally setting up an organization this way.

And yet, this is the default in many public and private organizations.

Now imagine working in that sort of ecosystem. Nobody is going to be focused on the positive things. Everybody's going to be focusing on the negatives, making sure we shed light on the negative elements of those above them.

This is why in organizations, you have to always make sure wins and losses trickle all the way down. If a leader is removed for a particular reason, everyone below him has to be removed as well—while looking at ways to retain institutional memory. This brings everyone onto the same team and promotes an attitude of working together.

If you do it that way, all of a sudden you build a sense of cohesion. They're all in the same boat. Everyone wins or everyone loses, so the department heads are no longer plotting to get that highest-level position but instead are focused on performance and delivery, raising the organization as a whole.

If you're aligned together, then the supervisor would automatically be on the side of the employee when the assessment comes in. They'd quickly figure out how to bring the employee up to a particular level of performance because it directly impacts their own performance metrics.

This level of commitment is crucial to the overall health of the organization. It means everyone is motivated to look out for everyone else.

The Truth about Whistleblowing and Flagging: It's Everyone's Job

Every individual's responsibility is to help ensure high performance *and* to quickly report if there is a performance issue. That will tell you which department or individual's performance to focus on, and this is easy once you have a performance structure in place.

They say in Toyota that any employee has the authority to shut down the factory. Press a button and everything gets shut down, because one small flaw in the system might create a costly ripple effect. But if something's wrong, employees are incentivized to catch and fix it, and if something can be done better, employees are incentivized to improve it. This puts power and motivation into everyone's hands.

These performance-only measurements help foster an open, competitive, and just environment, in the sense that people won't always come to you, because they already know to what standard they're being held. It's *not* a top-down, micro-managerial dictatorship that fosters division, mistrust, and suspicion. It's a bottom-up organization built on low-talent capabilities. This may differ from all the leadership models you've read about elsewhere. That's fine because those don't work in practice anyway. But Modern Alchemy does.

The registry, responsibilities, and rewards will transform your organization overnight. That said, we want more than just a quick win. We want long-term, sustainable success. Consistency. Without that, newly placed and motivated Associates revert to the previous, unacceptable mean, and bad habits resurface. We cannot have that.

The drum prevents this. We proceed there next.

Audit Your Responsibilities

1. Have you evaluated the responsibilities for every position in your company? Yes ☐ No ☐

2. Have you assessed whether or not each responsibility brings your organization toward its Due North (follow the Chain of Whys)? Yes ☐ No ☐

3. Have you eliminated **all** responsibilities that lead your company anywhere other than Due North? Yes ☐ No ☐

4. Have you rearranged your employees so that they perform roles that align with their traits (rather than their skill sets)? Yes ☐ No ☐

5. Does each role have a straightforward list of responsibilities and deadlines with a binary means of evaluating the completion of each task? Yes ☐ No ☐

6. Have you separated performance assessment from operations? Yes ☐ No ☐

7. Does your organization have an incentivized structure in place for rewarding performance and results that pursue or follow the company's Due North? Yes ☐ No ☐

8. Does your organization have a motivational system for whistleblowing to deal with problems that hold the potential to bog down or harm the company? Yes ☐ No ☐

CHAPTER 6

THE DRUM

Nothing big that is worth doing and that can change the landscape of an industry, or at times even the world, can be done alone. All projects require collaboration and coordination between great talents.

Therefore, if one cannot collaborate and coordinate, and if people can't work together, nothing great will ever be achieved or delivered.

Considering that Modern Alchemy deals with turnarounds and with the execution of purposeful projects that are worth working on, alchemy cannot exist if one does not perfect collaboration and coordination between the talents.

Marching in Unison and Harmonizing

Have you ever seen young cadets being taught to march in unison for the first time? It's a scene that is worth seeing, how individual steps start as a chaotic outburst of stomps and then, over time, start to harmonize through repetition.

If one compares the exercise on the first day with the performance on the last day of the training program, the change is phenomenal. You will see masters at work, throwing up rifles and walking in intertwined lines, all marching to the same step as if they are part of one whole.

This level of melodic harmonization is what you want to reach.

The reason it works so well is because everyone knows where they need to be. Everyone knows where everyone else is. Everyone knows their own responsibilities and, more importantly, when they will deliver. Everyone knows everyone else's responsibilities, what they are due to do, and when and where they will do it. With that level of clarity, individuals are no longer individuals; they are a part of a whole, and only when such a point is reached can greater things be achieved.

In organizations, it is the register of responsibilities that allows for these levels of predictability and therefore harmonization. Once an organization has completed the preparation and documentation of the register of responsibilities, everyone will know their exact role within your organization. This is not only related to what they will shoulder but also what they will do and when. They'll have a clear understanding of what they need to deliver, how their part connects to others, and how deliverables will be achieved and assessed.

For example, someone assigned to marketing in the registry who is tasked with creating new leads will understand that performance will be assessed by two criteria. Number one: the number of leads generated, and number two: the conversion rates of those leads into sales.

And your staff will be clear on their roles. They'll know whose job it is to drum up interest, who follows up, who secures the deal, and who executes.

The Drum Gives Structure to the Chaos

You cannot achieve anything big alone. In working as a group, there are clear dependencies, and someone needs to be able to communicate and coordinate the points in time where everyone needs to be and what they should do.

This is where the drum comes in. "Drum" is the short, broad term I use in my organizations to describe the rhythm and pace of work and all the associated dependencies. There must be something to keep everyone in step. Imagine a song without a beat. It would be chaos; the music would be unlistenable. Musicians and singers would not know at what moment to start, when to end, and so on. It is the same in organizations. The drum not only lets you identify *what* you're doing, but also *when* you're doing it and *what intensity* you need to be doing it with.

The drum means that everyone works at a steady, reliable pace with little to no unexpected delays. With roles assigned and responsibilities given, the drum answers the obvious follow-up question: "What am I supposed to do and when?"

In specific terms, the Modern Alchemist's drum includes **time**, **stakeholder**, and **dependency**. What has to get done by when? Who needs to be notified? Who is waiting for that work to get done? Those are the three key questions you should be asking when setting up your drum.

Example – *I, Pencil*

The 1958 essay *I, Pencil* asks us to consider what goes into the creation of a simple wooden pencil. The wood for the pencils must be harvested and transported. At the sawmill, it must be cut up into parts, and at the factory, these parts must be glued around the graphite core. An eraser has to be fastened on top, and then the pencils must be packaged and shipped to stores across the world.

While this process appears straightforward enough, in truth it is an amazing feat of cooperation.

Cutting the tree down requires multiple tools: saws, ropes, batteries, and so much more, all of which had to be manufactured. The sawmill where the wood is cut has its own set of machine tools, and those run on electricity that is generated at a power plant. The graphite for the point has to be mined, refined, and cut into its proper shape. The rubber-like substance for the eraser has to be fabricated and then carved to fit its precise space at the pencil's end. Every time something needs to be moved a long distance, vehicles must be used to transport them, and these vehicles must be fueled.[7]

All of that requires the talents of innumerable people, most of whom only know how to do just one step in the series of interconnected tasks. There is no way that a single human being could build, oversee, use, and maintain all the tools needed to make a pencil without relying on others. It would take a lifetime—many lifetimes.

This simple example of the pencil's creation reveals that cooperation is not some optional, sentimental nicety—it is an absolute necessity for getting anything significant done. Most of the people involved don't know each other, which points to another more subtle lesson: You don't need to have close friendships to have good cooperation, just a shared commitment to getting the job done.

---

[7] Leonard E. Read, "I, Pencil," Mises Institute, November 18, 2017, https://mises.org/library/i-pencil.

The key to this commitment is shared values. If all of you have the same general outlook *and* agree that the mission is worth pursuing, the practice of cooperation becomes easy. On the other hand, if your value systems clash too much, then cooperation grinds to a halt.

Example – Sales within a Public Entity

Let's see a quick example. If you work in sales at a publicly traded company, you're told in no uncertain terms that the conversion rate on your leads needs to take place smoothly throughout the year. Why? Shareholders of a public company are reported to on a quarterly basis. If they get a quarterly update that shows low conversion rates, they will get anxious.

This is, of course, very different if one were to have the exact same part in a private company. Such nuances are documented and shared within the register of responsibilities.

Now, imagine that you're confident you'll hit a deadline at the end of the year. But from the shareholders' perspective, their quarterly report shows the number of new leads and conversions as zero. For that first quarter, the share price will go down. If the next report doesn't show different second-quarter numbers, the share price will keep going down. By the third quarter, people will be jumping ship.

Even if you come through in quarter four and make your sales ahead of the deadline, delivery wasn't spread out over the year, which caused turbulence and chaos within the organization.

Managing the Orchestra

This is why we need the drum.

To continue with this musical analogy, picture your company as an orchestra. You wouldn't keep working with a violinist who skips training sessions, comes in at the end with an amazing solo, throws down their bow, and walks out. Without someone to play the violinist's notes throughout the remaining symphony, the music would fall flat.

Regardless of whether they are incredibly talented or not, the key to coordination and collaboration is predictability and consistency in delivery. If the output of an individual is not consistent, reliance on them by their colleagues will simply not take place.

Does this mean you need to produce constantly? The answer is no.

Think of a metronome. Its tick is steady and predictable, but it's not constant. It only ticks every so often, and if you happen to listen between ticks, you might think it wasn't working.

So what are the intervals that matter in your organization or your project? You need to know this.

Pointless, Continuous Spot-Checks

A lot of executives swear by doing surprise "spot-checks" to find out if people are doing their jobs constantly. But why should you care how often they're working if their performance is steady and predictable?

What I care about is performance at the intervals the company is performing at. Instead of doing pop quizzes that infantilize your employees and don't add value, inform them well in advance when they'll be tested and what they'll be tested on. Let them follow the ticks of the metronome.

They'll be prepared and it will keep the rhythm of the orchestra running smoothly.

Arguably, you should only care that the person is in the right place and delivering the right responsibility at the right time. What else they do with their time shouldn't bother you.

This is difficult to do, but one should always remember to ask themselves, *Do you want the performance, or do you want the effort?*

If you clarify which of the two you want, your people will cater to your wants and play to them. If you want a presentation of immense effort, people will project what you want and will show you extreme effort, at times gaming the system by exaggerating and creating complex scenarios. That said, if you are simply asking for performance at a set interval, your people will not focus on creating a silly narrative and politicking and will simply deliver the metric that you had asked for.

But the key to this is to be crystal clear or you will create a sick environment where manipulation reigns.

Beating the Drum in Your Organization

To implement the drum, two things need to take place. Number one, not only do you need to tell employees what you expect of them but you also need to spell out *when* you expect them to do it. Number two, inform employees which other stakeholders are relying on their jobs getting done. The guitar doesn't start playing until the drums establish the beat, so the drummer needs to know that the guitarist depends on him. Dependencies have to be crystal clear.

In a business example, the people responsible for follow-ups and lead conversion can't start work until those responsible for *getting* the leads do their job. The people in charge of executing contracts can't get to work until those responsible for conversion do. Internal auditors can't complete their tasks until those responsible for executing contracts are finished.

The drum unifies everyone with a time and date. What time and on what date is something due? "Every workday at 8:00 a.m., we . . . " or "Every Friday at 1:00 p.m., we . . . " or "Every last day of the quarter, we . . . " The drum gets people into a rhythm.

Those who used to be chaos and noise generators in the organization, going about with unchoreographed interactions, now know their place. They know which tasks to complete, the pace at which to work, who's depending on them, and whom to collaborate with—which authorities need to be reported to, for example. The result is tighter discipline and routine, a better rhythm, harmonic chords, and a beautiful tempo, if you will.

And the drum has relevance in the work-from-home question that many organizations are grappling with now: Do we allow work from home? If so, how often?

I hate working from home because of my more conventional ways. When I brought that up to a company I was working with, they asked me, "Do you want the performance? Or do you want the process?" They had a fair point.

Performance versus timed effort. Which is more important to the results you want? You need to know this.

The whole point is that what you want to identify is "what needs to be delivered" and "when it needs to be delivered." If you focus on those two key points as a minimum, you can leave the rest to the individuals to figure out.

Example – Prioritizing Effort over Time: A Construction Company Director Who Wants to Pay for Sweat and Not Results

As a relevant example, I was approached by a debt collection team that had a client who was the director of a construction company.

She came in when a customer owed her money and the deadline had come and gone.

The team had asked her to define her problem, and she reiterated that the customer didn't pay. She was coming to the service provider to get her the money she was owed. She was asked if she wanted anything else, and she said no, she just wanted her money. They agreed that she would pay the fee when she got her money. She signed the documentation.

Thereafter, the debt collection agency emailed her and said, "Good news, we got you your money. Could you collect it from accounts and pay our fee?"

She immediately contacted the company and me to make a huge fuss. She disputed the fee. "You never met with the counterparts. You never engaged litigators. You never registered anything with the authorities! The counterparts didn't even get a summons from you! You spent no time on this!"

Did she want the performance? Or did she want to see people sweat through the process? Those are two different things. If she had been clear with them that she was after buckets of blood and sweat, the agency could have exaggerated their efforts, delayed performance, and charged her accordingly.

In this case, all she told them was that she wanted her money, and money is what they delivered.

The reality of the situation was that the agency worked smart. They knew her customer. They knew who their bankers were. And they knew those bankers would not put up with a breach of contract.

In other words, the agency knew the audience that the counterpart was playing to. And when you identify someone's audience, you can, at times, forecast their actions and you can also know their pressure points.

So the agency worked on the pressure points. They just contacted the counterpart and said, "If you do not pay what you owe, we will issue a legal notice to your bankers—along with a request that they study your current credit rate." The counterparts paid promptly.

They were strategic, and they figured out the counterpart's weaknesses. Instead of doing the whole process of going through with notices, then appointing litigators and registering cases, the agency just got the woman her money.

What's the point of this story?

The construction company director was a Contractor, and Contractors deal with Associates. Associates get paid an hourly rate. So in this person's mind, the amount she was going to pay the agency needed to be linked to the amount of effort and time expended rather than to the final performance and value delivered.

And to her, effort didn't include mental exertion or capitalizing on previous experience and contacts, just buckets of sweat or long hours toiling away in meetings or sessions. She "forgot" she had signed an agreement to pay the agency simply for their performance: to get her the money she was owed.

She felt cheated—although she got what she engaged them for and at a speed faster than anyone else she had worked with before. But the reality is that she cannot think in terms of value. She is a Contractor who can only think in time and sweat.

Of course, the alternative interpretation is that she just didn't want to pay the fee and was making excuses to try to breach the agreement. I appreciate that it is very possible but, for this section and this example, that consideration is not relevant. Therefore, one gives her the benefit of the doubt here.

Humanity Wasting Man-Hours – Performance versus Effort

How does this apply to working from home? A work-from-home employee's priority is providing specific deliverables at specified intervals. Why did you need to see them in the office at six or seven in the morning? Remember to ask yourself: Are you paying for their blood, sweat, and tears, or are you paying to get a deliverable delivered at a given point in time?

Say you call your coworker, and you can tell from the sounds in the background that he's on a beach. Do you get agitated because he's not in an office? Or do you want him to give you the input you called him for in the first place?

Think about how many man-hours the world loses because of preconceived notions pertaining to how something needs to be accomplished and organizations' lack of readiness to challenge such preconceived notions.

Think about a kid taking a test. He goes into the exam room and finishes in twenty minutes instead of the allotted hour, so he just sits there. But the reason he's sitting there is not that he doesn't want to hand in the finished test. It's because if he were to hand it in, the teacher would be suspicious as to why he handed it in so fast. Even if the kid aced the exam, she may not feel he deserved full marks.

One wonders how much of humanity's existence has been wasted so far.

Chain of Whys

"That's how we've always done it." "This is what everyone else is doing." "This is in line with international best practices." "They [no one knows who they are] will not like this and it might impact us badly [no one knows how]."

Sound familiar? This is the sound of a failed enterprise and a failed executive team.

Now imagine an organization that gets rid of all preconceived notions and legacy steps. Imagine how much it can save. Imagine how much faster it can move. Imagine what ultimate synchronization can look like and feel like.

That's why Alchemists have the "Chain of Whys."

The whole point is that nothing is taken for granted, nothing at all. Each step, each assumption, and each assumed piece of logic is continuously rechecked. You get the idea.

This allows you to diagnose issues better. Here are a number of problems found through the use of the Chain of Whys.

Creating Useless Procedures and Rituals for the Benefit of the Audience

Think about the routine at a doctor's office. You visit and you're prompted to sign some paperwork. Then a nurse calls you in, puts you in a cubicle, and asks what's going on. You explain you have a temperature and a cough. Then the doctor comes to examine you with a stethoscope to hear your heart and your breathing.

Once, I asked a doctor colleague at what point in most such appointments he knew the diagnosis.

His response? "You said you had a fever and a cough, and I could hear your cough. So about six seconds."

"Then what is the rest of the appointment for? The measuring, the tapping, the testing, et cetera?" I asked.

"To demonstrate wisdom," he said to me.

Why? Because if you blurt out the diagnosis in six seconds, then tell the patient to take antibiotics and rest for a few days, the patient would go straight to management and demand a second opinion. So doctors go through the whole appointment ritual to get your buy-in. The patients' preconceived notions are just a waste. They're noise.

Imagine again how much of humanity's shared experience is lost to legacy structures, legacy procedures, legacy assumptions, and legacy arrangements. The typical personification of this is, "This is how it's always been done."

Now imagine how much value is unlocked and efforts saved when one moves past such sort of legacy thing. In this case, one need only look at what telemedical services have done to the world to appreciate just how impressive the amount of time saving really is. The "lucky" ones are the ones who decided to remove the shackles of the past.

Time Spent Preparing Excuses and Playing Defense

Think about a typical child procrastinating when it comes to "useless" homework. Think about the time that the student assigns to come up with an acceptable excuse that would allow him not to do the work without being penalized. The usual examples include "the dog ate my homework," "house emergency," and so forth.

Imagine how much of humanity's existence has been wasted on this as well.

When you ask for a status update, the "responsible" person will often say, "I'll check with so-and-so and get back to you." That's a gateway to assigning blame, finger-pointing, and deflecting responsibility.

Further, it sets these brilliant players up to play the role of wise and honest "advisor," where they proceed to update you on what the imaginary *they* (the unnamable ones) did wrong and how your proverbial "wise and honest advisor" has been conscientiously and selflessly following up, but the matter is not in his hands, seeing that he is powerless and merely a messenger.

Needless to say, when you come across this situation, the unnamable *they* magically perform when they are named, and the wise and honest advisor performs when they're reminded that they are executives with deliverables and not advisors.

You will find these "advisors" all over your organization.

When dealing with them, there is still hope. When one minimizes opportunities for them to update you on the excuses, and once it sets in that they need to perform and that their work has impact on the output of their colleagues, "advisors" tend to turn back into executives and perform.

This is particularly true when one limits upward reporting in line with the dam, as we will see later in the chapter.

"I'll Do X, Okay?"

It's interesting how the world is the same but in different colors wherever an Alchemist undertakes a project.

On each project, before we implement Modern Alchemy's strict upward reporting protocols for any project, we always see executives using a tried and tested legacy trick. They would report as follows, "We're going to do X, Y, and Z," or "We'll do X." Then they'd say, "OK?" as if asking permission.

If one provides a positive response, Alchemists would have been demoted from Alchemists to supervising Contractors. Why is this dangerous—and humorous? Because the trick is a genius defensive measure intended to minimize repercussions when targets are not met without the timeframes placed. This works because as an active participant in the failed effort, the Alchemists cannot now assign blame fully and transparently without sharing a significant portion of the blame.

If you've ever served on a board of directors, you'll know what I mean and you'll have seen endless examples of this from the managing executives. Although you and the rest of the members know that the vast majority of the board's job is talking strategy, the fact of the matter is that most boards spend their valuable time discussing items that management doesn't want to take responsibility for and instead pass up the chain of command for someone else to deal with.

The purpose of the dam and restrictions on upward reporting is to minimize success when it comes to these political games.

Reinforcing the Dam with the Five Types of Upward Reports and How to Use Them

We've already established that the harmonization of team effort through repetition and through systematic coordination is a definite objective and target for any organization that is serious about thriving.

For one to reach that level of harmonization, the communication needs to be purposeful and needs to be distilled to what is absolutely necessary so that interruptions are minimized as well, allowing deep work and real focus to take place.

That said, the key issue is that the vast majority of people work on some sort of basic salary structure which naturally entices one to focus on time and effort instead of performance. What is also another natural outcome is that because people are not remunerated based on the responsibilities they shoulder, the risk they carry, and the value they generate, it is natural that many people would try to minimize their exposure and the number of decisions they take on behalf of the organization, therefore minimizing the risk on them and their jobs.

For that reason, a clear phenomenon appears where decision-making requirements are naturally pushed up from the front lines to the corporate offices and the top of the organization. This is clear to see when one considers the tendencies to micromanage (and at times nano management) that the seniors are required to adopt at times to ensure that matters are executed in the right way.

This tsunami of queries and requests for decisions from the bottom up is what needs to be stopped if an organization is going to be successful in harmonizing. This thereby limits senior management's input to key strategic decisions only and allows the remaining members of the organization to shoulder the decision-making process within the set parameters.

It is for this reason that we refer to the construction of a proverbial "dam" to slow down the wave of requests that juniors send up the organization, thereby minimizing the noise and allowing more coordinated, performance-driven activities.

The Gates within the Dam

There are **five** types of upward reports and communiqués that are allowed in Modern Alchemy. Adopting them will guarantee minimizing the amount of noise and intrusion for the benefit of all the talents within the organization.

Type 1 – FYI (SYDHIFO)

The first is the **FYI (So You Don't Hear It From Outside)** report. This is the information feed that is expected of all organizations and team members, where they inform the superiors of relevant information that has taken place—without passing the ball.

The reason for the emphasis on not passing the ball is that historical data and experience tend to show that parties tend to send in FYI reports, therefore implying that responsibility for the flagged matter has been passed over to the superior.

This is not how Alchemy works. An FYI report cannot be perceived to be a handover of responsibility or even the approval pertaining to sharing the responsibility. The responsibility, as per the register of responsibilities, is shouldered by one person only and cannot be shared through FYI reports.

Therefore, the "For Your Information" reports are issued with a huge qualification. They're saying, "I want to inform you so that you don't hear this from outside, *but* I'm still fully responsible for this and I'm handling this. Nothing is needed." Without that "but," an FYI report shirks responsibility.

These reports are simple reports. The information flows upward because you think those above you should know this information. That's all. You're still solely responsible.

Type 2 – Request for Authority

The second type is the **Request for Authority** report. This is used where a decision needs to be taken with regard to a particular matter but no one within the organization seems to have the authority to make the decision.

One needs to remember that one of the most challenging elements of Modern Alchemy is that the Alchemist may not "touch the ball" and therefore cannot make any executive decisions other than to set the Due North and pick and incentivize the talents.

In our organizations, although actions are audited, we seldom give authority to those requesting it. We've found that it is best to set out the logic of where the authority rests, ensuring that the authorized person is wholly aligned with the organization.

To be clear, a Request for Authority is not a request for a person to be granted the authority. Instead, it is supposed to identify why someone has the authority to make a specific decision.

Type 3 – Request for Policy Clarification

The third type of report is a **Request for Policy Clarification**. It means that the sender wishes to ask a transparent question and needs clarification with regard to the Due North, functions, responsibilities, key deliverables, SOPs, or similar queries, but may not relate to a specific action or decision that is due.

This type of communiqué can also be a request to amend a target, a policy, or an SOP. These types of documents support documenting matters within the organization.

Request for Policy Clarifications must be in writing, where the issued must set out clearly what the question is and what they believe to be the answer. It is important to establish what the issuer of the question thinks is the right policy from the very beginning to better understand how bad the misalignment is.

Type 4 – Red Flag

The fourth type of report is the **Red Flag**. This type of report is used when an employee has observed something that will impact the organization negatively and should be reported immediately. This report should rarely be used, as one of the keys to a successful organization is to limit the number of urgent matters that interrupt senior management.

This report, when used, should trigger an "all hands on deck" meeting, considering the seriousness of the matter that has been reported.

Type 5 – Dropped Flag

The final type of upward report with the dam system is referred to as the **Dropped Flag** report. Simply put, this report is issued by talents when they know what the Due North is, when they have been assigned and know what the shouldered responsibility is, and when they have the authority required to fulfill it, but for some reason, they cannot (or will not) execute the project or responsibility.

Needless to say, when such reports are self reported, it tends to (but does not always) mean that the talent is not in the right place or that they are not able to continue to shoulder a responsibility.

Example – Traffic Police and a VIP

There was an American propaganda Cold War joke said by US president Ronald Reagan which perfectly reflects the situation where a Dropped Flag report is issued. I've paraphrased President Reagan's joke as follows:

> "An order went out one day in the Soviet Union to the police that anyone caught speeding was to get a ticket, no matter who it was. President Gorbachev was late one day leaving home and getting to the Kremlin. He told the driver that he [Gorbachev] would drive and so the driver sat in the passenger seat. As he drove, he passed two police motorcycles while he was speeding. One of the police motorcycles went to stop him.

"When he got back to his partner, the second policeman asked the first if he had given the man a ticket. The first policeman said, 'No.'

"The second policeman asked, 'Why not? They told us to ticket any car that is speeding.'

"The first policeman answered, 'He's too important. I couldn't.'

"So, the second policeman asked, 'Who was he to be too important to be ticketed?'

"The first policeman answered, 'I don't know, but he must be incredibly important. He had President Gorbachev as his personal driver.'"[8]

In this skit, the character of the first policeman definitely knows the Due North. He has his directions, he knows the policy, and he has the full authority to stop the vehicle and ticket whoever was in it, but he opted not to—presumably because it's too much confrontation for his pay grade.

He is willing to follow the policy and to execute up to a particular level, at which point he opts out. This is the perfect time when a Dropped Flag report would be issued.

The key to the drum is to maximize coordination, minimize interruptions, and maximize the empowerment of specialists. Applying the drum to your organization will provide the necessary pace with which your organization will be performing.

---

[8] President Reagan's original joke can be viewed at https://www.youtube.com/shorts/EUKPUXDdWNE.

Audit Your Drum

1. Have you clearly communicated to employees what you expect of them and exactly when you want it done? Yes ☐ No ☐

2. Do your employees know which stakeholders within the workflow are depending on them to get their jobs done? Yes ☐ No ☐

3. Have you emphasized the superiority of performance over effort within your workplace culture? Yes ☐ No ☐

4. Have you assessed which steps in a task's completion are merely "for show" and which are actually necessary, then eliminated the ones that are for show? Yes ☐ No ☐

5. Have you assigned appropriate responsibility to lower management tiers to protect upper management from wasting time on decisions that don't need their input? Yes ☐ No ☐

CHAPTER 7

THE TALENT

Entire organizations, industries, and even countries can rise on the shoulders of an Alchemist. We've all seen it. But can they do it all alone? The simple answer is no.

The most important element within Modern Alchemy is the people, meaning the team. It is the understanding that one person cannot scale or cross generations.

Therefore, the most important element is the "talent," as named in our lexicon. These are the individuals who report to and support the Alchemist. Without these people, there would be no performance, no choreography, no gold, and no ripple effect.

Modern Alchemy is designed to address the needs of a team, an organization, a company, a department, or even a community that is about to go through a miraculous turnaround. This is not a solo herculean effort; it's all about teamwork.

In all cases, the talents all have two things in common. The first is that they consist of voluntarily cooperating and collaborating individuals; the second is that they are led by one Alchemist who establishes direction, membership, roles, and responsibilities and who is the final ultimate arbiter of performance.

Further, one needs to understand that there will be no voluntary cooperation or collaboration, no cross-pollination, and no win-win propositions if the values are not shared by the members and if trust does not reign between the individual members of the community. This is why transient, limited-term political interactions do not lead to cooperation or collaboration. Transient relations focus on zero-sum arrangements while trust-based, shared value, collaborative recurring interactions are based on long-term mutually beneficial arrangements, elevating all who are involved.

It is for this reason that anything and anyone that lowers or negatively impacts trust within the talent pool must immediately be removed and at any cost. Synthesizing trust—trust amongst team members and trust in the system—must reign supreme in the priorities of the Alchemists.

The best image of this example is when picturing the famous Belgian draft horses, who individually, it is said, pull in the range of eight thousand pounds. But when joined together, the two horses don't pull sixteen thousand pounds, but instead pull twenty thousand pounds. That said, when you join two together who have trust in each other and who have been raised and trained together, the pulling capability of two horses can reach up to thirty-two thousand pounds. This is incredible when one considers the difference in output when trust exists between two collaborators.

So, when selecting, always give priority to long-term, recurring relationships and interactions rather than a short-term, transient relationship. The returns are higher over time and the incentive to support each other and honor one's word is clearly evident.

Simply put, the talents are the most important elements in Modern Alchemy. And in realizing that, one needs to also realize that the talents will not react positively with each other without the trust that emanates from the individuals' shared values. One must therefore select well.

In dealing with talents, the challenge is to never judge a book by its cover and to always control being influenced by preconceived notions about individuals or groups. Let the individual's actions show you who and what they are, and when they show you who they are, believe them. I cannot emphasize enough how difficult it is to do this and how much control and discipline the Alchemist needs to have to be able to protect themselves from influence and projections of past experiences onto a talent.

One of the best examples we've seen of where the Alchemist reads talents' abilities and limitations pragmatically comes from sport, an example that I would recommend to any serious student of Modern Alchemy. The example is the one found in *Moneyball: The Art of Winning an Unfair Game* by Michael Lewis, who analyzed the real story of the Oakland Athletics baseball team and their magnificent feat and turnaround brought about primarily through reading ability and configuring strategies and positions on the field without being influenced by "the book's cover."

Only the best Alchemists are able to judge talents objectively for who and what they really are by reading their actions and their achievements and assessing their abilities.

When assessing individual talent with the Modern Alchemy method, some labels are helpful, but binary statements (good/bad, high/low, etc.) are not. One must always remember that things are relative and must be seen on a spectrum and are not always binary.

Ask a manager or a supervisor how they really feel about their staff, and you'll probably hear an earful about "low" performers and "bad" employees. After a few (or several) minutes of venting, they'll realize that they don't sound like inspiring leaders and will therefore switch gears. The tune will switch to "good" employees and "high" performers. One reason is that confronting the issue at hand requires resources and energy, both of which may not be available at this time. Besides, it does not impact the manager directly, so why address it now? Then, they'll share an anecdote about a star worker they had groomed, a story that will cast them, the proverbial leader, in a positive light so they can enjoy the credit themselves. This type of insight through verbal observations is not helpful for the talent, the organization, or the Alchemist.

Such random statements about individuals are neither helpful nor beneficial, which is why Modern Alchemy prefers limited labels. This allows one to divide an organization's workforce into groups and camps, to manage interactions, assess potential, and focus on upskilling and improving performance, boost morale, and grow the organization for the benefit of all.

So, while other books may tell you the type of worker you "should" hire or "should" inspire your team to be, here we will chase no such fantasy. Modern Alchemy deals with reality—what is, as it is. We chart it as best we can and ask ourselves, "Now what?"

In this chapter, you will discover the types of talent you find yourself surrounded by in your quest to turn organizations into the best-in-class versions of themselves.

I'll warn you, this next section may be painful because you might come to unwanted realizations. It may be inspiring. It may be both. The key theme is the old adage goes, "Lead, follow, or get out of the way."

In the next few pages, you'll learn who in your organization needs to be empowered to lead, who needs to learn to follow, and who needs to get out of the way.

The Talents Alchemists Work With

When turning an organization into a gold-making, highly efficient performance machine, one always starts from the top and never, ever the middle or the bottom. Although we've seen examples where changes from the bottom or the middle have been partially beneficial, the rarity of their success and the sheer amount of effort required make the investment and the allocation of time and energy simply illogical. Therefore, we will not go through those technical maneuvers in this book.

An ancient proverb, "The fish rots from the head down," is perfect for understanding the logic of our start. Always start from the top and work your way down. It's more efficient, seeing that the very first task would be to correct the organization or team's direction. And logically, change from the top has a cost-effective, beneficial ripple effect, minimizing resistance throughout the organization even before any specific changes are made.

So, before you do anything, the Alchemist must be in place. Once in place, the Alchemist must observe his team members and categorize the talents into seven categories. These categories will dictate how much responsibility and decision-making authority is entrusted to each and their proximity to the decision-making and policy-setting core.

Who You Should Never Bother With

Before an Alchemist even starts to work on the organization, assess it, or start the recruitment process, an investigation must be undertaken with regard to one trait in particular that individuals have. This will dictate whether the talent is even worth considering.

It is not whether the talent has the necessary skill sets. It is not whether the talent has the necessary networks. Simply put, it is whether the talent was historically a good or bad leaver from the previous organization.

Bad Leavers

All organizations, all associations, all affiliations, and all projects are, by their very nature, impermanent. In all cases, individuals are brought together for a purpose and will one day move on to something else.

The validity and applicability of that truth to all talents is the reason why the person's traits with regard to how they transition from one organization or from one project to another, regardless of the reason, are simply the most important part of the selection process.

An Alchemist will never work with anyone who has been seen to be a bad leaver or a destructive leaver in the past, simply because people are habitual in nature and tend to repeat what they do.

What you're looking for is someone who, even in the worst of times when there is a disagreement or they may have even been terminated without cause, still honors the sanctity of the relationship even when others don't. This ensures that all matters are handed over in a state and through a process that exceeds the employer's and colleagues' expectations.

What you need is an excellent, stellar leaver to safeguard the institution that you're building together when the inevitable parting of ways takes place, whether it's due to retirement, divestment, termination, or any other reason.

Simply, nothing is more important for the longevity of an organization than to have good and excellent leavers within its midst.

Who Leads

It goes without saying that the individual who leads the organization is the Alchemist and only the Alchemist, without any interference whatsoever. The "buck stops with him" and only him (or her) in all matters relating to the organization. An Alchemist takes full responsibility for all the good and the ill that happens in the organization, and such weight cannot be delegated to anyone else's shoulders.

Of course, the patrons or the community that has engaged the Alchemist does have a choice in dealing with the Alchemist. Choice number one is to allow the Alchemist to do his job as he deems necessary based on his experience and expertise. Choice number two is to remove the Alchemist and replace him with someone else.

Interference or influence after the engagement is out of the question. It is bad for the organization, bad for the talents, bad for the patronizing group, and bad for the Alchemist.

Once that's clear, one must always remember that an Alchemist cannot and must not be on the proverbial "field" and cannot ever "touch the ball" during a game. Therefore, the Alchemists need uniquely qualified individuals on the field who can act as their agents and ensure that prioritized matters are addressed and tasks are completed.

Generally speaking, it is always best to find such talent from within the organization. Very rarely are such talents not available somewhere within the many hierarchical tiers of the organization, if the organization is large enough. Only if they are not found internally should external talent be brought in. Otherwise, the emphasis must be on identifying, grooming, and promoting internal talent.

Now that we understand that the Alchemist leads, let's meet the agents who support in leadership positions on the field, where the Alchemist is not welcome.

In this section, there are two types of team members, **Contractors** and **Partners**. They're similar but also different. We'll go through the traits together.

It is essential when selecting Contractors or Partners to ensure that both have a very low time preference, being willing to sacrifice today and immediate gratification for greater future gain.

It is also crucial to always remember that for one to be a Contractor or Partner, they have to show that they need absolutely no day-to-day observation or support in handling their responsibilities. None, whatsoever. Otherwise, they are neither Contractors nor Partners.

Type A – Contractors

"Contractors" in the Modern Alchemy lexicon are the individuals who are given a "group priority" to safeguard and are able to safeguard without any interference, support, or oversight from any third party, especially the Alchemist. Simply put, if the individual needs hand-holding, editing, or supervision, he is not a Contractor. He is possibly an Associate but definitely not a Contractor or a Partner.

The key differentiating factor between Contractors and Partners is that Contractors have a predefined duration and are transient, preparing to move on eventually from the organization. Partners, as we will see, are aligned with the organization and its outcomes for the long term.

Contractors have resources under their control, including other Contractors, Associates, equipment, finances, and whatever other requirements are needed to get the job done, depending on the situation at hand.

Under no circumstances is a Contractor to attempt to blame a failure on a staff member or any other third party. The Contractor is solely responsible for protecting the prioritized matter and ensuring deliveries at the pre-agreed times and dates. The Contractor must be weary of delivering on time considering the linked dependencies with his colleagues. Dropping the flag will disrupt their work and interrupt the performance of the organization. Dropping the flag is out of the question.

You had heard previously that the Alchemist plays an infinite game. That is true at that level within the organization or the team. The Contractor plays a finite, be it longer-term, game. The Contractor tends to handle a portfolio and deals with delivering recurring priorities and items.

His eyes must be "on the ball" or the responsibility at hand. To reiterate, the rule is simply never drop the flag. The whole organization is depending on him.

Needless to say, an Alchemist has many Contractors reporting to him, each focusing on a designated priority.

Let me give you an example to better support the illustration. Imagine if you had a horse racing team. One Contractor may be assigned with the priority of handling logistics in moving the horses safely and comfortably from their current location to the racecourses, and to do so in a manner that ensures that scheduled requirements are met. This Contractor will be solely responsible for the horses' welfare when en route, for managing the expenses of such logistical operations, for selecting the routes, for clearing the cargo, for arranging the veterinary support during the trip, and so on. This burden is never shared. It is carried by one person.

That is not to say, of course, that the steps and the technical matters may not be delegated to other parties. They may, but the burden is never delegated and never shared. And in delegating, the Contractor has sole discretion, considering that he is solely responsible for delivery—but that does not excuse him from the need to explain decisions clearly to the whole group. Remember, if he corrupts the delegation of the responsibility process or if he corrupts the trust within the organization due to nepotistic preferences or other corrupting forces, this will impact the performance of the whole. Therefore, all key stakeholders and counterparts should be informed of the decisions and the clear reasoning behind them.

One must note that Contractors may, at times, report to other Contractors and may be delegated with deliverables within set or restricted parameters. The key to the matter is to always remember that Contractors are delegated responsibilities and audited but never supervised.

After the Alchemist, Contractors and Partners are the backbone of any organization. Identify these individuals correctly and you're on the path for some magical changes.

A prime example of a Contractor who made a high-stakes career move is David Beckham. After achieving incredible success in Europe with Manchester United and Real Madrid, Beckham made the pivotal decision in 2007 to leave European football behind and sign with LA Galaxy in the United States. This move wasn't just about a temporary change or a short-term deal; it also reflected Beckham's calculated decision to build a global brand and explore new opportunities beyond his prime playing years. Although his contract involved significant financial gain, Beckham's decision also allowed him to secure equity stakes in Major League Soccer, showcasing a Contractor-like mindset where he leveraged his skills while keeping his options open and avoiding a permanent, long-term commitment like a Partner might.

Type B – Partners

"Partners" in the Modern Alchemy lexicon share almost all the traits of the Contractors, as they are deemed to be mature Contractors. The main difference between the two relates to the level of long-term commitment, where Partners have to be wholly bought into the organization or the enterprise. Their future interests must be interwoven with the interests of the organization.

Partners cannot be dealt with at arm's length only, as their net worth, career prospects, and future safety is bound to the team or the organization in a manner that is difficult to untangle. Of course, with each type of organization, the manner in which this binding is done depends on the legal structure of the enterprise. In companies, it would be through equity ownership. In politics, it would be through party seniority and alliances. In sports franchises, it would be through long-term contracts. Each has its own separate nuances.

These are not individuals who are hedging their bets. Partners are all in—fully committed to the organization, the team, and the "tribe." They embody the direction and the values adopted by the organization. They are wholly bankable in all matters needed to the Alchemist.

As the Alchemists are never "on the field," the Partners are the eyes and ears of the Alchemist and provide the real core agency. While the final decisions are the Alchemist's, the Partners' opinions carry more weight than any other category.

Predictably, Partners may report to other Partners. Contractors can also report to Partners. What is less predictable and somewhat counterintuitive, Partners can also report to Contractors, particularly when Contractors are more informed and more able in a particular skill set.

That said, Modern Alchemy always calls a spade a spade. Partners are titled as such and Contractors are identified separately to clearly differentiate between those who "are all in" versus parties that are hedging or are more transient in nature. This is essential to safeguard against misalignment with the long-term direction.

A modern-day example of a Partner is Jony Ive, Apple's former chief design officer, whose relationship with Steve Jobs highlights the essence of a true Partner. Ive wasn't just a highly skilled Contractor but also someone whose future was deeply entwined with Apple's success. His long-term commitment went beyond a job title—he chose equity over higher salary options, a decision reflecting his deep alignment with the company's vision and future. Ive's creative direction, much like a Partner in Modern Alchemy, was fully bankable, and his opinions held more weight than anyone else's in the organization. Steve Jobs even referred to him as his "spiritual partner," further demonstrating how fully Ive was committed to the organization's long-term success. He became a vital component of Apple's identity and values, helping shape the company's core products, from the iMac to the iPhone.

Who Follows

We've gone over who leads and have established the skeletal backbone of the organization, namely the Alchemist, the Partners, and the Contractors. We will next need to add the support functions that assist in realizing the purpose of the organization.

While the previous group leads, these two separate types of team members follow and support. They are the Associates and the Advisors. This group is essential and does much of the heavy lifting. More importantly, this group provides the Contractors and eventually the Partners of the future.

Type C – Associates

Associates provide a support function and are immediate reports under the Contractors or the Partners. The Contractors and Partners are fully responsible for the output of the Associates and may recruit them at their discretion.

The key difference between the Contractors and the Associates is that the Contractors require no supervision whatsoever, while the Associates require the Contractor's supervision and support.

Associates tend to be higher in time preference, thinking primarily of the here and now and, at times, of the immediate future, but not thinking nor acting for the long term. Contractors do think and act for the longer term.

When assessing time preference, think of the marshmallow test. This test was a social experiment undertaken by a professor at Stanford University back in 1970 and revolved around delayed gratification. The theory was that individuals who were willing to delay their gratification, work today to benefit tomorrow, were more likely to succeed. The experiment tested children by giving them a piece of marshmallow. The children were allowed to either eat it there and then or wait with the prospect of gaining a second marshmallow in a few minutes if they showed self-control. The experiment seemed to prove that the ones who showed control and waited moved on to have much better life outcomes in the future—better educations, better lifestyles, better health, and so forth.

Although the experiment itself was challenged with other experiments in later years, the concept is sound and logical. The conclusion is that wherever possible, recruit and promote Associates who show the ability and readiness to delay gratification. They will be better Partners and retain more value as they grow.

On another note, Associates have lower skills than Contractors. Their costs are usually lower as well.

Associates are usually tasked by Contractors to handle more time- and effort-intensive responsibilities to allow the Contractors to focus on resource allocation and quality assurance. Needless to say, Contractors remain fully responsible for Associates' day-to-day output.

It is the Contractor's responsibility to identify the Associates' skill sets or natural abilities and push them in that general direction, playing to their strengths until such time when they are elevated to the realm of Contractor with their own mandates.

Type D – Advisors

Whereas Associates are temporarily low on knowledge and have limited responsibilities, carrying minimal amounts of the overall burden, Advisors are high on knowledge and skills yet have no responsibility whatsoever and carry none of the burden.

There is a huge difference between the two that Alchemists must know. While one may be reliant, the other is wholly transient and apathetic. This leads to very different outcomes and very different perspectives.

Note that current and aspiring Advisors are the most common of the types we are analyzing in this book. Only on the rarest of occasions is one truly able to benefit from their in-depth knowledge of a specialization. To do so, Alchemists must really know what they want out of the Advisors and should have a strong grasp of the subject matter as well.

Generally speaking, it is usually best to retain external Advisors on a contract, either on a case-by-case engagement or on a general retainer of sorts, where the Advisors serve others and also serve the organization when needed. Their interaction with more than one organization usually allows Advisors to stay up to date with respect to their craft or core expertise, which ends up being a win-win proposition for all.

Contracts also make it crystal clear that the relationship between the Advisors and the organization is a transient one and that therefore, their input is taken with the necessary grain (or more) of salt.

That is not to say that Advisors are not beneficial; they can keep you informed about what is happening in a given sector.

Every once in a while, one finds an Advisor with a specialization that is close to the core of what the organization does. As such, that Advisor becomes an indispensable resource, providing independent, informed, aligned, and deep advice. When that Advisor is found, retaining them to support Contractors works very well and may add significant value and insights. That said, the rarity of such a find cannot be overstated, so one is best advised to outsource the arrangement and transact at arm's length without burdening the organization with recurring costs.

The key concern usually with Advisors is the mismatch and misalignment of interests between the interests of the organization and their personal interests. When serving internally, they are not incentivized to appreciate the urgency of matters and also tend to complicate matters instead of simplifying them. It usually takes a significant amount of effort to try to find an incentive structure that would fix this disconnect.

To conclude, never forget that Advisors do not carry the burden of the organization. They are good to have, but at arm's length and for very specific mandates.

Who Should Get Out of the Way

The third element in the old-quoted saying relates to who should "get out of the way." This is the easiest of all the types to identify. Ridding the organization or team of these types does wonders to the organization and its momentum.

There are three main types in this section that should be addressed, namely the Thorns, the Shamans, and the Divas.

Type E – Thorns

The Thorns are the most blatantly obvious of all the types of individuals and should be the easiest to identify. When you enter a new organization, everyone usually already knows who these are. So, listening goes a long way, but any leads must be tested properly.

We had previously discussed the organization's direction and its values, the red lines that this microcosm of a community will not cross. These are the things that leadership within the organization will not do, regardless of the positive impact such action would have on the organization's direction or current state. These are lines that one will not cross. Each organization has different lines, but some may be "never misreport" or "never steal."

The Thorns, simply put, are individuals who do not share these values. They do not share these red lines. They will do what the organization will not.

With such misalignment, there is no choice but to work to release such individuals from the organization or team. The key reason is that they neither generate trust nor collaborate with other members. They become a bottleneck for all matters and cause significant disruption.

Contractors and Partners simply will not rely on Thorns because of the value misalignment. This, in turn, leaves them with very little to do. One finds that they are neurotically nano-managed by their supervisors, which leads to significant waste. This becomes very disruptive.

Even when Thorns are not damaging to the organization, they become a burden to the group and start to create a sense of inequity and animosity which is neither healthy nor necessary.

Sadly, Thorns don't fit and must be removed. There's no other alternative.

Now, this should not sound as a surprise to anyone, if one had been following the logic behind the definition closely. Just because someone is designated as a Thorn in one organization does not mean that they will not fit perfectly in another organization. A Thorn could readily disagree with the values of one organization and agree fully with the values of another.

Therefore, the trick is to help the Thorn find an organization whose values match his. The removal process is not always painful and, if done correctly, the Thorn would be grateful for the change.

Type F – Shamans

One piece of advice that will help you with your future endeavors is to be wary of Shamans, especially corporate or institutional Shamans.

When joining an organization in an effort to turn it around, you will come across a type that is the hardest to identify. They come in the shape of Advisors, Associates, and, at times, even Contractors. What sets them apart is their extreme attachment to dogma, their extreme attachment to what others are doing, their extreme attachment to what people have done in the past, and their almost prophetic conviction that the organization cannot change and will not deliver what is intended.

Shamans are peddlers of fear, uncertainty, doubt, and disbelief. Their impact on the group is usually negative, to say the least.

The difficulty with Shamans is that as Associates or Contractors, they sometimes go through the motions and perform the acts that they need to ensure that they retain the role. That is why they are so difficult to identify.

The reason we refer to them as Shamans is because of their reliance on fear and superstitions in herding individuals into taking a particular position and doing so quietly without too much controversy or much fanfare. These are the ones who spread discontent and distrust without rising to the forefront to identify themselves and state their positions and views publicly.

One needs to be careful not to mistake Advisors for Shamans. Some Advisors in certain instances advise caution, and rightly so. But they do so based on logic and a depth of understanding of the material at hand, not on fear and drama as Shamans do.

The key difference that helps in identifying whether someone is a Shaman or an Advisor is that an Advisor will speak their peace in a private setting confidentially and in front of the decision maker and then speak no more of the matter outside. The Shaman rarely speaks openly and usually focuses on whispers amongst the lower tiers of an organization, causing disruption in the buy-in of the overall organization.

Simply, real Advisors never attempt to rally individuals quietly and are never populists at heart. They advise Contractors, Partners, or Alchemists and provide their insights to them only and in a formal format. Shamans, on the other hand, focus at times on politicking, which just wastes time and resources and weakens the whole.

Shamans are usually inherited, kept in place by Contractors or Alchemists who don't know enough about the processes at hand, the specialization, the market, or the organization's intricacies. The only reason they are kept in place would be because a Contractor, Partner, or Alchemist is worried about moving an unknown variable.

Shamans, with their fearmongering and superstition, add very little value. They simply gnaw at the organization's unity and faith in their direction.

The sooner they're out, the better it is.

Type 6 – Divas

It is true: Superhumans exist. Just one person can change a team's performance; they score all the points. There are some out there that have superhuman talents. They are incredible. Their achievements are brilliant. These gems are wanted and needed in a perfect world.

Sadly, it is extremely rare for you to be able to find or recruit these insanely successful or insanely productive individuals, particularly when dealing with failing organizations that you're trying to turn around. Very few are willing to join a sinking ship in the hopes that it may be salvaged and they would be able to share the upside. This is particularly true if the project happens to be in a third-world or developing country.

It's even rarer still to find these superhuman talents with a stable head on their shoulders, without undue appreciation for their personal grandeur. Many are narcissistic at the core, full of entitlement. Their inclusion within the organization, regardless of their individual scorecard, tends to lower the performance of the whole organization.

Superficially, the numbers would show that the organization is doing better in the short term with such superhumans, while the reality is that the remaining team members get weaker with time, considering the excessive reliance on a single person.

Superhumans with a "me, me, me" narcissistic mentality and a wholly mercenary, transient, contractual relationship are referred to as Divas in the Modern Alchemy lexicon.

Divas are the easiest to identify. Switch on a camera and watch them change, they become transfixed. If the junior talent is interested in being on camera or in the press constantly, their focus is not on the organization but on marketing themselves. If this person keeps issuing odd, immaterial press releases and statements in an attempt to be noticed, you've found yourself a Diva.

The problem with the Diva is that they have the exact opposite effect that yeast has, figuratively speaking. Whereas yeast raises the whole and makes the sum more than the parts, Divas cause the community of talents to shrivel to less than the sum of their parts.

Modern Alchemy counterintuitively tells you that normal talents will do just fine without the Divas, regardless of their superhuman abilities. The team just has to be extremely disciplined and work together institutionally, each knowing their role and their individual deliverables and coordinating and cooperating seamlessly.

Modern Alchemy is clearly of the view that Divas aren't worth the headache. Because of the sheer depth of knowledge available with an Alchemist, assuming you can get (or become) the right Alchemist, you'll have somebody who segregates priorities and responsibilities in such a manner that mirrors the Diva's abilities, keeps everyone else on track, on point, and on message without the drama and turbulence that comes with having an actual Diva.

If done properly, you can get surprisingly excellent results and improvements even from talents whose previous leaders thought incapable of performance. You will very quickly not even realize that the Diva is missing.

Notice that at no point in the book have we discussed individual superstars, Divas, and how they will single-handedly carry the team to glory. The reasons are simple: They're not needed, they're not wanted, they're not sustainable, and their benefit is limited and at times exaggerated.

Consider Travis Kalanick, co-founder and former CEO of Uber. Kalanick is a strong example of the Diva archetype in the Modern Alchemy framework. His ability to propel Uber into a global powerhouse was undeniably impressive—his vision and drive led to extraordinary growth. However, as is often the case with Divas, Kalanick's leadership style was marked by a focus on his personal brand and media presence, which at times created friction within the organization. While his contributions were significant, his dominant personality and high-profile approach introduced challenges that impacted team cohesion. Kalanick's example highlights how even the most talented individuals can shift the focus from organizational success to personal achievement.

The magic of Modern Alchemy can be done without the use of Divas. You're actually better off without them.

A Brief Sports Example

Let's go back to sports. Say you're the new incoming coach of a previously losing franchise.

You start with fixing the team's regiment, sleeping patterns, eating habits, travel schedules, and other protocols and routines until each player is as healthy as you can make them. Then, you start to identify the specifics of each individual, figuring out their types, the burden they can carry, the responsibilities that fit their traits and abilities, and the roles they should play. You focus on building their muscle memory through repetition and continuous choreography of particular tasks.

Once you've done this for even a brief period, you will realize that even with sub-superhuman talent, you can achieve peak performance if their synchronization is perfect and if you're playing to individual strengths. This is because hard work with proper direction quickly becomes indistinguishable from innate talent.

You don't need "top performers" to drive organizational greatness. The job of the Alchemist is to orchestrate, call plays, conduct, and write the recipes that make for a top organization. Simply put, Alchemists design, create, and work through systems.

Once you set the direction, communicate the Due North, adopt the values, segregate talents, and identify their roles and the burden each can carry, you will start to surprise even the inner team with the magic that comes to fruition and the increased performance.

Finally, allow the Divas to transition out while keeping a steady stream of talents coming into the organization. This sounds very similar to what Sir Alex Ferguson did with the Manchester United franchise, shocking the world time and again by releasing Divas and continuing to win without losing a beat. This is an example worth researching.

On the other hand, Bahrain did just that with its national football team starting in 2018, and the change in performance was phenomenal. The whole sector was very proud of the achievements and felt privileged to have seen the transformation firsthand.

Iterative Evolution

So, you now know about Alchemists, Contractors, Partners, Associates, Advisors, Thorns, Shamans, and Divas. The natural reaction will be to move and act quickly, especially if the organization is on a seemingly downhill trajectory. With the information that you have now, one might assume that you should immediately fire all Thorns, Shamans, and Divas, demote Associates, and promote Partners and Contractors.

Please don't. Not so fast.

Remember that organizations work like living and ever-changing organisms and not solid structures. Remember also that Modern Alchemy is an iterative process where one makes one change and waits for it to settle, waits for the remaining parts to recalibrate and get rebalanced, then takes the next step and so on. You're not dealing with a mechanical structure where you make all the corrections in one go and assume that it will run smoothly. Physics and force allocation do not apply in the social engineering fields.

The truth is that the process is more like chiropractic maneuvers and physiotherapy than mechanical interventions. You would make the correction, give it time to heal, allow the blood to flow, allow the body to move, and then make the next one when the patient is ready for the next correction.

Organizations act very much like living organisms where when one element is changed, there is a whole web of interconnected relationships that need to organically and naturally re-collaborate.

So, whatever you do, do not come in and make all the changes in one go.

The reality is that the definitions provided previously may misrepresent reality when they're oversimplified and interpreted by individuals who are not Alchemists. Alchemists know that Thorns are not always Thorns and that Divas are not always Divas. Some Divas' traits melt away as soon as a strong competitor joins the organization. The same applies to other types. All talents are on a spectrum of such traits. All talents continually change their state depending on the environment, their perception of the future of the organization, their individual role within an organization, the level of appreciation, and the overall trajectory and opportunities.

The reason that one starts with corrections at the top is to allow the impact of a correction to ripple through the organization; to allow the talents to recalibrate and reassess their options, their interests, and their alignment with their organization. One may readily find a Contractor who elevates to Partner, or an Associate who transforms into a Contractor, shouldering part of the burden. A talent may also be a Shaman but then becomes a Contractor.

These types are not set in stone. They indicate risk levels and reliability which may impact the productivity of a given organization.

Therefore, it is always essential to remember to never superimpose your past hopes or prejudices on a current reality, for that is a sure recipe for failure, if not disaster. The key to Modern Alchemy is to assess the reality of the situation for what it is and not what you wish for it to be. Assess talents for what they are right now, because they change over time, and not what you wish them to be.

Therefore, continuous reassessment is essential.

Your team members will show you who they are if you'll allow them. Never impose unnecessary, excessive expectations that could get in the way of that. Little continuous tests like this activity instead show you what you can expect of your talent in the short term.

As an Alchemist or would-be Alchemist, your focus must be on your talents' abilities and reliability. You want to retain talent where the deviation over time is minimal to allow you to rely on them for growth and scale.

Sadly, non-Alchemists typically focus on what organizational personnel do not know how to do well. That misplaced attention results in a negative feedback loop—*I keep giving you work you don't know how to do, you do it poorly, I micromanage you, you complain, your performance decreases,* and so on. Instead, one must only focus on what talent can do, and do repeatedly.

There is no underestimating how important talent is in Modern Alchemy. There is no gold without the team, and so understanding the team members is paramount prior to any success.

Audit Your Talent

1. Have you categorized all individuals in your organization into one of the six types of talent (Contractor, Partner, Advisor, Thorn, Shaman, Diva)? Yes ☐ No ☐

2. Have you taken steps to get the Thorns, Shamans, and Divas out of the way? Yes ☐ No ☐

3. Have you started at the top and worked your way down? Yes ☐ No ☐

CHAPTER 8

THE INNER LIGHT

A quote that had stuck with me for a while was one I heard from Charlie Munger. He was asked, considering his success and old age at the time, if greed really did make the world go around. His response was, "The world is not driven by greed. It's driven by envy."

Think about that for a second. Think about Charlie Munger's enlightening statement.

Envy
(noun)

- a feeling of discontented or resentful longing aroused by someone else's possessions, qualities, or luck

This reminds me of the research by Frans de Waal with regard to how even the non-human brown capuchin monkeys (*Cebus apella*) respond negatively to unequal reward distribution in exchanges with human experimenters. They refuse to participate if they witness another participant obtain a more attractive reward for equal effort, an effect amplified if the partner received such a reward without any effort at all.[9]

De Waal thinks that people may not just be estopped from participating but, in the inverse, may also be driven by the same feeling of discontent stemming from what others possess or receive, which they do not. If true, and if all organizations are people organizations, then this variable must be a key consideration to keep in mind when incentivizing.

That said, I would add one more element, more importantly: Not only is envy a strong driver, but the aspiration to be envied by others seems to also be a dimension that is alive and well. This is evidenced by the mania that is social media and the eternal quest for the acquisition of [envious] "followers" through the publication of surreal and touched-up selfies.

If the premise is true, such a quest for equality in the first instance or the quest for envious followers in extreme instances is a reality that can be utilized to positively guide a person's actions. This can be used by an organization and an Alchemist through the use of what we refer to as Inner Light.

People's Actions Differ When the Light Is On

Every organization is a people organization first and foremost, whether we like it or not. And all people are seemingly unpredictable, if one is being honest in his assessment, simply because none of us know all the different variables that are influencing any one individual, be it nature, nurture, or current circumstances.

---

[9] https://www.nature.com/articles/nature01963 and https://www.youtube.com/watch?v=fZ7LwYPiA1I

Simply, you just don't know whether or not a person would act honorably, ethically, or contractually. Sometimes, people not only act in breach of the covenants of the contracts they have made with you, but they may also seemingly act in a manner that is even self-destructive. You simply don't know.

That said, what we do know is that the vast majority of individuals seem to be social beings who care about the opinions and acceptance of others. They want others to look favorably on them for acceptance, for security, for prestige, and for followers.

The reality is that one important dimension that one does not take into account is that people play to an audience; they play to the court of public opinion.

Therefore, the logical conclusion is for all organizations to ensure that the leadership retains a tight grip on the use of the proverbial stage and, more importantly, controls the light shed on a talent within an organization.

This "Inner Light," as we refer to it, can create extremely impactful yet soft parameters or boundaries that can positively limit the negative actions of individuals and, in certain circumstances, even positively impact the actions of individuals.

Shining the Inner Light

The Inner Light (and the corresponding stage) is an excellent tool used by Alchemists and should be entrusted to only the most qualified of operators. But this is a dangerous tool. Many careless aspiring Alchemists have met grisly ends because of errors in use.

This light is like fire—a good servant, but a terrible master. And much like a fire, if you let the power of such light's concentration run unchecked, your organization will be burned out, just as much as if a blaze had consumed your offices.

For a demonstration of where this can lead, look at social media. While major social networks like Facebook, Twitter, and Instagram have moderation rules, these do not include prohibitions on pressure campaigns. As a result, entire groups gang up on one individual whenever that person says something out of step with the spirit of the age. The extreme example, of course, is the "cancel culture" phenomenon.

An Alchemist must always remember that you can try to guide the narrative, but you can never fully predict the world's response or the reaction of masses and stampedes.

That's why your organization must retain complete disciplined control over the Inner Light. Alchemists can control the intensity of the light, like a small candle, then a gas stove, and then a raging inferno.

The Inner Light can, of course, be used at indifferent intensities for positive reinforcement or for negative corrections, but the one matter that remains true is that different intensities can lead to different reactions.

Here are some examples of the lower- to higher-intensity use of the Inner Light within organizations.

One-on-One Verbal Interactions

One-on-one interactions are the first step on the Inner Light's intensity scale. This provides talents with an audience of one, letting the talent know that someone is watching and recognizing what is being done—whether good or bad.

As is the case with all uses of light, it can be used as a reward or as a correction.

When using such levels of Inner Light, always avoid vague language such as "we" or "us." It's *you*, the talent, and *me*, the supervisor. One must also be crystal clear about what action is being rewarded or corrected.

When this is first used, the impact on the actions of talents is quite surprising, considering the effort involved in the quick one-on-one verbal interaction.

Small Internal Group Intervention

The second level on the Inner Light's intensity scale is a small audience or colleagues within the organization.

This usually entails a ceremony or ritual meeting to officially review and therefore recognize or correct actions that have been undertaken by talents. Such interactions tend to be formal in nature and include documentation of such interactions.

The formal nature of the interaction and the permanence of the records associated with the interaction grant a much higher degree of intensity for such action.

The rituals associated with the intervention are very important, including where the interaction takes place, who is in attendance, and how the interaction is being recorded.

This tool is significantly stronger in intensity to individual one-on-one interactions and therefore should not be used generously.

Organization-Wide Recognition

The next level of intensity on the Inner Light intensity scale is organization-wide recognition or corrections. Both types are quite potent in their impacts and both provide a much larger audience base.

The key differentiator here is that the community as a whole would be involved. The inner court of public opinion is one that constitutes the whole community of peers whose adoration and respect the talent tends to aspire to gain.

In addition to that, the ceremonial nature of the interaction and the permanence of the records pertaining to the interaction tend to magnify the impact on the talent.

Such tools tend to be beneficial not only for altering or reinforcing actions but also for curating and grooming the future actions of others within the community who are undoubtedly watching closely.

Public Recognition

The next level on the Inner Light intensity scale is the administration of recognition or correction publicly. In positive terms, this usually refers to medals, Talent of the Year awards, public promotion, and the like. In negative corrective terms, this can be demotions, terminations, court cases, public investigations, and the like.

In all circumstances, these public, permanent interactions must be administered in a highly restricted and controlled manner to ensure that the impact received is the intended one.

This sort of interaction usually requires significant effort in drafting and controlling the narrative that is to be consumed by the public audience and therefore increases the complexity of such matters. Therefore, the messaging has to be crystal clear on why the individual is being rewarded or why they are being reprimanded to ensure that there is no ambiguity.

Example – United Arab Emirates Government

One of the best examples that one comes across with respect to the use of Inner Light to publicly set the tone of the organization for promotional and corrective aims is the example of the initiative of His Highness Sheikh Mohammed bin Rashid Al Maktoum, the prime minister of the United Arab Emirates, in publicly declaring the best and worst performing ministers and administrations[10] within the government apparatus. One can only imagine the impact such actions create.

His Highness made it a custom to periodically publish the respective performance assessments and findings which immediately corresponded with actions, including promotions, terminations, and issuance of warnings with strict rectification deadlines.

The fact that such actions are done so publicly and in such a transparent manner creates the intended ripple effect within the overall organization—in this case, the UAE government apparatus.

The assessment of the performance of the ministers and their respective leaders is done such that there is no ambiguity whatsoever within the talent pool on why a change was made, why something was celebrated, or why individuals were deemed to have failed to perform.

Such actions, done publicly and at the very top of the organization, send a clear message about the meritocracy that is being honored, the direction that is being followed, and the expectations one may reasonably have.

Legend-Building

The final level on the Inner Light intensity scale is what Alchemists refer to as the "legend-building" process. This is the storytelling, narrative creation exercise that solidifies the lessons and messages that are meant to have been indoctrinated into the DNA of the organization.

The key to such affirmations is to communicate to an audience the selected background pertaining to circumstances and

---

[10] https://whatson.ae/2023/11/sheikh-mohammed-reveals-best-and-worst-uae-government-services-2023/.

then focus on the decision-making and the overall outcome of such action or group of actions.

There is a public permanence associated with this level of intensity, whether it is reward-based or an intended deterrent.

Every organization has legends and institutional memory, but very few of them control what is being emphasized or the clarity of the message that is embedded within the legend.

Therefore, it is essential that an Alchemist picks and reinforces the legends that he wants to cultivate with the use of the Inner Light.

Shed Light on Dependencies

Organizations are armies. They have to gear up at a specific time, define the parameters of their mission, and attack it with all available force. For the mission to be completed, everyone must perform their tasks as planned. Like in real wars, no plan survives first contact with the enemy, so the organization must change plans as needed. And to top it all off, lives are at stake, as hundreds of people's financial futures ride on the organization's success.

Vague goals and objectives won't work. If you have high stands of performance that those under you can't shirk or weasel out of, you have to demand specific deliverables by specific times. Hard requirements and deadlines shine a light on who in your company is performing and who may be holding things up.

And it's not always underperformers holding up progress. Any employee or Contractor with dependencies—others dependent on their work—can put everyone behind schedule when a deadline *cannot afford to be missed.* This isn't laziness from the worker; it's just a natural consequence of that person's job.

Shedding Inner Light on deadlines and dependencies makes poor performers obvious. All the blame games, the politicking, and the finger-pointing stop at once. There is no arguing with a lack of results. You either met the goals or you didn't.

Even better, this dependency means you're not the only one motivated to push the failing employee. Everyone else downstream will give that person an earful, and he'll have to either improve or disappear. Light brings clarity not only to your eyes but to your organization as well.

You and your colleagues will all know instinctively and unambiguously who are the sources of the bottlenecks and who are the pillars of the organization.

Audit Your Light

1. Have you set up a system to identify when and where Inner Light is needed? Yes ☐ No ☐

2. Have you put a process in place to differentiate between the different intensities of Inner Light? Yes ☐ No ☐

3. Does your company have a method to keep personnel matters internal, dealing with them at intervals: first one-on-one, then a small group committee, and then within the greater organization committee? Yes ☐ No ☐

4. Have all your employees been made aware of your organization's "red line" behaviors (boundaries that they cannot cross without losing employment, the favor of the company, or both)? Yes ☐ No ☐

5. Have you selected and reinforced your legends? Yes ☐ No ☐

CHAPTER 9

THE DRAG

Now that positions, tasks, and deliverables are clear, you can stop doing all that previous busy work. Just stop; I mean it. Upward reporting takes unnecessary tasks off your company's plate so you can do less. What I'm about to teach you may feel extreme, but transforming subpar talent into greatness usually is.

Imagine running with a large kite behind you. The resistance will provide you with an excellent workout, but you'll go a short distance with great effort. Organizations raise kites behind them and keep them there for years. In this chapter, we'll remove the drag behind yours. In a few short pages, there will be nothing to hold you back any longer.

Now, what does it mean to "do less"? It doesn't mean to get lazy but to eliminate drag on your organization instead. When you have your people in positions aligned with their personalities and strengths, certain tasks will no longer be necessary. And the beauty of doing less is that fewer resources are required. Your organization becomes lighter and more efficient because of it.

By now, your Due North should be crystal clear. Due North examples from my work include creating more hope for youth, more predictability for justice, and more opportunities for Associates.

Having identified your Due North, you'll now work backward to establish your priorities. Then you'll continue backward to lay out your responsibilities and deliverables. That's backward planning.

The first step to doing less and working smarter is to place all your tasks on a matrix. It's what I call the *What Next?* matrix.

The Chain of Whys: How to Stop Moving South (Or East or West)

After you set the Due North, it's time to start filtering out with the Chain of Whys. Most likely, you're not dealing with a new organization. When things start to change, you have to ask, "Why are we doing what we're currently doing?"

It's easier to stop doing what doesn't take you in the direction you want than it is to try new things. We realized this at the Ministry of Youth and Sports, which is why we changed our direction to "gold only."

Look at the events on your calendar and your team's calendar. Ask, *Why is our team doing this?*

The Chain of Whys reveals all the ways that you're taking yourself farther from where you want to go.

The Chain of Whys Identifies Drag in Education

Let's look at education again. In the West, school starts around 7:00 a.m. and ends between 2:00 and 3:00 p.m. Why? So parents have time to commute to work once they get their kids out of the house, and so teachers have time to grade assignments before the end of the business day.

If that's correct, let's clarify: Who are the customers? They clearly aren't the students. They seem to be the parents and the teachers seeing that the service benefits them the most.

How do you know this to be true? Studies have shown that the later school starts, the better kids do. And if you start with physical education in the morning, the return on their academic performance goes up even higher. So, if the students were the customers, surely, the school timing would cater to whatever grants them the best outcome.

Data also shows that covering a day's worth of lessons takes only a fraction of the current school day. There, "US public education" seems to be a misnomer, seeing that providing a safe environment for childcare or babysitting is a large part of what is being provided.

In other parts of the world, they use a much more accurate term for such systems. They have a Ministry of Upbringing and Education. "Upbringing" refers to the childcare element, which takes prominence over the educational and upskilling element in the title.

The relevance of this analysis is to identify the Due North clearly and establish whether the responsibility that is being executed and that is taking up resources moves the dial in the direction that is needed or not.

If one uses the Chain of Whys methodology, can you imagine how much is being done within the realm of this example that can be cut out? Which resources can be reallocated to other matters?

I've seen a recent example of a youth program that allows children to congregate and trade within a safe space and with adult supervision. This is like a large physical marketplace with booths that are made available to youngsters, which allows them to swap, trade, and sell.

Imagine how much can be learned by youth from these interactions with regard to young financial literacy, interactions with others, contracts and trade, assessment of value, future planning, and other skills—while still keeping the kids in a safe place until their parents come to collect them.

Exercise – Linking Your Chain of Whys

Sit down with every employee and ask as many "why" questions as necessary to find the real answers. Get explanations, and keep asking "Why?" Use the Chain of Whys to figure out why things are the way they are.

Why do you have a media department? The answer you might get is "Because every company needs a budget for that." Well, Tesla claims they don't have one, so why do you need one? Keep asking these "Why" questions to get down to the bottom of why you do things the way you do.

Following the Chain of Whys will help you cut out unnecessary activities that are wasting time and resources by leading you in a direction that you ultimately don't want to go. Remember, it's easier to stop doing something that's resisting the future state than to start doing something new. Start with the easy stuff. I'll show you how exactly to do this in Chapter 9. There, you'll learn to use a helpful tool that tells you which Due North–distracting activities to eliminate. This will help you proceed faster toward the future state you desire.

The *What Next?* Matrix, Part I

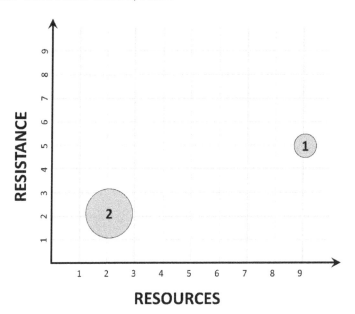

	Initiatives	Resources		Resistance		Impact	
		Money 50%	Staff 50%	Approvals 50%	Rivalry 50%	Revenue 50%	Exposure 50%
1	Operating the new branch	8	8	2	8	0	4
2							
3							

0 – 3 Low	4 – 6 Medium	7 – 10 High

Start by opening a blank document and creating a table with four columns: Initiatives, Resources, Resistance, and Impact. In the Initiatives column, list every project your company is currently undertaking.

Now, let's assess these initiatives on a scale of 1 to 10. Take, for example, a new branch your company has opened. While this branch may be costing a significant amount and requiring a substantial allocation of staff, it's also facing tough competition in the area. Despite not generating revenue, it provides valuable exposure for your brand. When you plot this initiative on your matrix, you might find it has high resource consumption (let's say an 8), medium resistance (around a 5), but low impact (perhaps a 2). This means you're investing heavily for minimal returns, classifying it as a drag project.

To gain even clearer insights, you can break down the Resources column further. Consider adding sub-columns for specific resource types, such as budget allocation, staffing hours, and even marketing expenses. This way, you'll have a detailed view of where your resources are going, allowing you to institutionalize this approach and make more informed decisions about which initiatives to prioritize or cut. By systematically analyzing your projects in this manner, you can focus on those that truly drive value for your organization.

You'll soon identify activities that are burning through resources, causing a lot of friction and yet having little impact. You can also ascertain which activities are **low-resource, low-resistance,** and **high-impact**. I confer with my colleagues about keeping new initiatives in the low-resource, low-resistance, high-impact matrix. I plot these tasks as circles. Your aim is to work in *this* area of the matrix as much as you can because it gives you the maximum return on your investment.

How many of the actions in the **high-resource, high-friction, low-impact** area can you simply stop doing? You'll want to avoid working in this section of the matrix as much as you can.

Let's look at some examples of low-impact situations you want to avoid.

High Resources—High Resistance—Low Impact

These are white elephant projects—mega-projects that are expensive and just for show. You're only doing them because someone in authority said so.

Think about rebranding. It's expensive and seldom has much impact. The effort usually takes people and resources away from jobs that have a higher impact.

Consider hosting paid guest speakers at events. Hosting events often costs a lot in speaking fees. Then the speakers use their talks to stir up drama, which keeps people from delivering on their responsibilities.

Some speakers at work events charge $20,000 for a ninety-minute talk that does more to divide the company than to unite or empower it. Whether it's a critique of leadership or an absence of diversity, it often leaves employees feeling worse about themselves and resentful of their coworkers. This is a high-resistance initiative. Be very careful when assessing the impact of your guest speaker.

Guest speakers aren't always high resistance, nor are they always low impact. You might get a guest speaker who talks about shortcuts they've found in the industry and therefore focuses on quick upskilling and re-skilling employees in quick brief interactions.

Either way, your Associates run the risk of wasting time through events like these. You don't want that. Nor do you want them wasting money, as we'll see next.

High Resources—Low Resistance—Low Impact

These projects are expensive to get started. People will do them without a fuss, but they seldom accomplish anything.

A good example is building a new headquarters. If it's expensive and doesn't do anything, why do so many firms build new HQs? Because it's an ego trip.

Think of the Apple Infinite Loop campus. Nothing about it makes business sense. After all, Standard Oil had a magnificent campus, and they're defunct. But Apple's CEO wanted the Loop and had the trillions to build it. High resources, low resistance, low impact.

It's unlikely your organization can afford such a pricey vanity project. And no one can afford poor employee morale.

Another example is IBM's 1956 project in which the early computing company set out to build what would at that time be the fastest supercomputer in the world. They took five years and produced the IBM 7030, called "Stretch." Although it was very fast, the computer failed to meet its original goal of being one hundred times faster than the system it was replacing. This forced IBM to drop the price they had planned to charge for Stretch, which then priced the computer below its manufacturing cost. This led the company to eventually stop selling the supercomputer altogether. In the end, this was a huge expenditure of time and resources that ultimately had little impact on the market, with less than ten sales made for these supercomputers.

Low Resource—High Resistance—Low Impact

These are tasks that cost little yet don't achieve anything. What's worse, they frustrate your employees.

Mandatory workshops are a great example. They take up time your sales teams could be using to make sales calls. Instead, these people lose hours a day. These workshops only impede Associates from doing their jobs, as they now have less time and are still responsible for their deliverables.

Another example can be seen in the ubiquitous staff meetings that take up massive amounts of collective time when the same thing could be achieved by everyone reading a concise briefing and ensuring they understood all of its content and what it meant for them. Perhaps you've seen the bottle of hand soap next to the sink that poses the comedic command, "Wash away useless meetings… read the damn email!" Meetings that waste time are often met with resistance from employees, whether on a conscious level or not. It's common to find employees who feel they can't get their important work accomplished because they have to attend so many meetings a week.

Low-resource, high-resistance, low-impact activities like these just get in the way of work that needs to be done and can stand in the way of important connections, focus, and even breakthroughs for an organization.

The next section of the matrix isn't as bad but still puts a drain on your organization and should be minimized.

Low Resources—Low Resistance—Low Impact
These are tasks that cost little, nobody cares about, and have little effect, yet they're still being done. This is like the proverb, "Death by a thousand paper cuts."

Welcome meetings for new people fit this category. Social committees do too. You might throw little celebrations or give shoutouts in the internal newsletter for employee birthdays or even get the cheapest available cake. But does anyone remember once that last piece is gone? If it's not significantly boosting employee morale, you might as well save the cake budget.

Whether it's buying the company lunch or sending a mass mailing of generically-signed holiday cards, it's important to allocate the resources to the activities that employees care about. Employees might rather skip the catered lunch and have a gift card, which means less administrative costs.

The above examples are items you could cut to better allocate resources to the things that have a significant positive impact on the employees and organization. Any time you remove anything that causes drag, you increase your organization's momentum toward your Due North direction. Remove whatever creates resistance, and you go that much faster without exerting any additional effort.

Imagine a cyclist. The less drag their bicycle, uniform, helmet, and other gear create, the faster they naturally go. There's an art, but more so a science, to minimizing every vector of wind resistance they possibly can in order to be the most aerodynamic cyclist they can be. The fastest cyclist wins. Most often, that's not the one with the strongest legs and most muscular build, but the cyclist with the least drag to fight against.

Now, what about those golden low-resource, low-resistance, high-impact projects? That new effort, those new initiatives that will be worth far more than any resources expended? We'll explore that in the next chapter.

Audit Your Drag

1. Have you created the *What Next?* matrix for your organization? Yes ☐ No ☐

2. Have you found and eliminated all activities that fell into the low impact section of the matrix for your company's Due North? Yes ☐ No ☐

CHAPTER 10

THE OPPORTUNITIES

The previous chapter focused on identifying and stopping the Drag, or the waste and drain of resources that is going toward unimpactful projects or procedures. If this was done correctly, this would arguably mean that all things being equal, you now have a tremendous amount of saved resources, time, and energy that can be reallocated to higher-impact projects.

I understand that the segregation of the two chapters, namely "The Drag" and "The Opportunities," makes it seem like one stops the whole operation. Does "The Drag" say to audit, then reallocate resources, and then restart operations again? Clearly, that is not possible in reality. Everything is done in parallel. What little resources are saved by cutting drag projects is immediately reallocated to higher-impact projects.

All that needs to be done is for the energy, time, and resources that were going to a low-impact project be reallocated to a higher-impact project.

Key Risks

There are two primary risks that need to be addressed at this interval, namely decision paralysis and agreeableness.

First Risk – Decision Paralysis

Note that we referred in the previous section to "higher impact" and not the "highest impact." This is done purposely. Many people have a risk of decision paralysis when shouldering the responsibility of finding the absolute "best" allocation of resources, time, and energy.

One needs to always remember that although the options may seem infinite, the time one has to make the decision and find the opportunity is very finite. Note that sometimes more damage is done by omission than by action.

Alchemists do not search for the absolute best solution, nor do they freeze in the process. Alchemists are searching for a "better" solution than the one currently being applied. The word "better" is key to understanding the mindset.

It is essential to also realize that Alchemists believe in the iterative nature of things, that you make decisions based on the information and abilities that you currently have and may iterate in the future. The amount and quality of information, the types of abilities, and the availability of resources all change over time, which leads to more insight and unlocks opportunities that previously seemed impossible.

Second Risk – Agreeableness

Now that one has the time, energy, and resources that may be reallocated to new projects and initiatives, it is essential that one remembers that although time, energy, and resources are now available, they are by no means infinite and must be allocated carefully.

The biggest problem that one finds when revisiting such situations is peer pressure from customers, colleagues, and stakeholders. Many tend to fall into the trap of initiating new projects or initiatives being requested by others in an effort to minimize confrontation, without really assessing the resources required or the impact.

At other times, worse yet, some reallocate the resources to new projects or initiatives simply because others are doing the same.

Think about it. How many times have you seen resources being squandered just because others have done the same? Think about how the United States Postal Service actually funded a cycling team in the Tour de France. How many of their end users even know that the Tour de France exists or care? Why would they do that? Examples of such illogical allocations are endless.

Therefore, having a clear, strict, and rigid project initiation process that assesses the true impact of proposals is key.

Setting Up the Project Initiation Process

The most important element of Alchemists' work is the use of purposeful actions, meaning that all actions, prior to being undertaken and prior to resources being expended, should be considered, analyzed, and assessed.

The Muslims have a beautiful phrase that best embodies this, namely that "acts are gauged by their underlying intention and purpose." Such ideology forces reflection prior to any act or omission. Therefore, every act or omission should have first been considered, analyzed, and assessed.

When assessing a prospective project or initiative, three key parameters must be taken into consideration, similar to those covered in the chapter on the drag: the resistance and complexity of the initiative, the resources required (including time, funds, facilities, etc.) to execute the initiative, and the impact such initiative will have.

Defining the Impact to Be Measured

It is key to remember that in any Modern Alchemy project, the impact that is being gauged is not always the same. It differs from project to project and from Alchemist to Alchemist. That said, the impact always stems from the direction.

When the direction of the organization is to have "more gold," then the impact being measured must relate to the gold. When the direction of the organization is to have "more employment," then the impact being measured must relate to the employment opportunities being created. When the direction of the organization is to increase its "real book value," then the impact being measured must be the growth in the organization's treasury.

In each project or undertaking, the impact that must be measured is different. Identifying that impact is key to the success of the endeavor.

Low-Hanging Fruits, Matrix, Part II

In whatever field or industry they may work, there are golden opportunities, or low-hanging fruits, that Alchemists want to grab. The easiest way to identify them is to reflect the opportunities graphically to assess their differences.

In preparing for the analysis, Alchemists tend to have a live document or a live database that is continuously amended to chart the opportunities. Three main data points are graphed, which support the analysis and selection process prior to initiation: complexity (resistance), resources (time, facilities, and money), and impact.

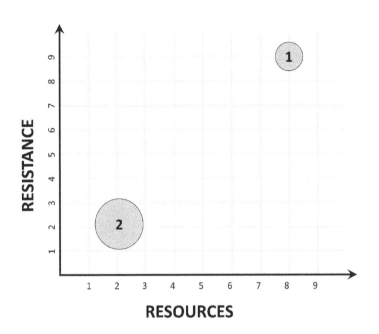

	Initiatives	Resources		Resistance		Impact	
		Money 50%	Staff 50%	Approvals 50%	Rivalry 50%	Revenue 50%	Exposure 50%
1	Opening a new branch in MENA region	9	9	8	7	0	2
2	Signing collaboration with XYZ company	1	1	4	2	8	8
3							
	0 – 3 Low		4 – 6 Medium			7 – 10 High	

Referring back to the *What Next?* matrix, this essential tool can also be leveraged to pinpoint golden opportunities or identify the so-called low-hanging fruits.

Consider two initiatives currently under review. Project 1 focuses on an independent product launch, requiring substantial financial resources and a large team. This initiative brings with it high levels of complexity and uncertainty, with questionable impact on future revenue. In contrast, Project 2 centres around a partnership for a co-developed product with another company. This initiative demands a more modest budget and only a small team. Despite lower resource requirements, the potential for revenue and increased market exposure is far greater.

When mapped on the matrix, the difference is clear: Project 1 consumes significant resources while offering limited returns, whereas Project 2 stands out as the low-hanging fruit—minimal resistance, fewer resource needs, and substantial impact. This makes it the clear choice for pursuit.

By applying this matrix, Alchemists can efficiently sift through competing initiatives and concentrate on those that best align with their strategic goals, ensuring the optimal use of resources and minimizing unnecessary risks. Keeping the matrix dynamic and regularly updated with new opportunities is key to continually uncovering the most favourable pathways forward. The tool is very well suited to allow Alchemists to visibly identify and compare opportunities.

What is important to remember is that the tracking device is a live database, because the three data points change over time. Something that was expensive—such as IT, for example—becomes cheaper over time, whereas complexity and resistance change over time depending on the political and social realities and the buy-in one gains or loses over time.

There are many examples of where projects made complete sense all the way up to launch only to have the winds of change alter the reality on the ground, forcing the project to be stopped. The opposite is also true. This reality is why we need a live organic document or database.

That said, once the document is available, analysis and allocation of resources become much easier. This tool will assist in finding the low-resistance, low-resource, high-impact initiatives that are worth investing in.

Example of a Low-Resistance, Low-Resource, High-Impact Project

Remember the Hope Fund I mentioned previously? Our Due North was to create the environment, interest, and excitement to allow for startups to be created and have them aspire to reach unicorn status.

The Hope Fund had a number of initiatives over the years, but we had noted that the pace with which we were marching towards our Due North was lacking. We needed a low-resistance, low-resources, high-impact project to start to speed up the momentum.

Simply put, we needed to drum up excitement among the community, investors, and shareholders by showing that transactions were taking place, that opportunities were rampant, and that there was vast wealth to be made if everyone rowed in the same direction.

At that point in time, as is the case in most settings, the waters of the SME and VC world within the immediate region seemed somewhat stagnant. We needed to create some high-impact ripples to get things going. We were hoping that if we muddied the waters just enough, we would statistically generate a few good wins for the SME sector in the Kingdom of Bahrain.

So, we used the low-hanging fruit tool. One option stood out and was implemented: create a streaming TV show to shed light on opportunities and deals.

We created a media show called *Beban*—which is Arabic for "doors" or "opportunities"—on a shoestring budget to showcase various entrepreneurial startups who present their ideas and ventures, thereby competing for investments on the show. The show also allows the audience at home to invest as well through a special app. The investors decide which venture they feel has the best chance of success, and if lucky, the entrepreneur gets the award of securing funding for their business.

Our show shed light on current investment opportunities, starring current Bahrain investors and highlighting the uniqueness of their business models and innovative ideas. It grew to have participation from around the Arabian Gulf states and beyond. The show was intended to be local, but it became so popular that it became the number one show in the Middle East on Shahid (the regional equivalent to Netflix) and gained a region-wide following.

Inspired by the mission of the show, people started to contact us, excited and eager to discuss investment opportunities for their companies and themselves. Potential investors started calling us because they'd seen the show and were intrigued. They wanted to appear on an episode as one of the "investors" to support local businesses.

This mania reached a whole new level when, during the third season, we added a new spin: *Beban Juniors*, where kids as young as five years old and as old as seventeen were inviting to pitch their business ideas before the panel. You can imagine the reaction. The kids were natural stars, and the community rallied behind them.

There is a clear before and after in the impact the show had on the landscape. This was the perfect example of a low-resistance (and complexity), low-resource, high-impact project that hit the mark.

Sourcing Opportunities and Initiatives

Examples such as the success of the *Beban* show are not a daily occurrence. It is not every day that one comes across a clear low-resistance, low-resource, high-impact initiative, so one should not stall if those are not readily available.

The idea behind the low-hanging fruits tool is to support in identifying the differences between the initiatives and allow one to select the path of least resistance. For that reason, one must always keep the tool populated with as many opportunities as possible and should periodically track the three key dimensions: resistance (and complexity), resources needed, and the impact of the initiative.

It is key for this to succeed not to assume that this is a top-down mechanism. It is not. Most, if not all, of the initiatives must be generated from the community of informed stakeholders and not from the top. Therefore, having a mechanism for opportunity identification and recommendation by staff, partners, shareholders, end users, and even vendors is essential.

The role of the Alchemist is not to know everything and propose, plan, and execute all initiates. The role of the Alchemist is to independently study the opportunities and initiatives and decide whether resources should be allocated or not.

Audit Your Opportunities

1. Do you have an ongoing mechanism to collect recommendations for opportunities and initiatives? Yes ☐ No ☐

2. Do you have a tool to assess the resistance and complexity, the resources needed and the impact of such initiatives? Yes ☐ No ☐

3. Do you know what impact you are measuring for? Yes ☐ No ☐

4. Do you realize that there is no perfect answer and therefore one should not suffer from decision paralysis? Yes ☐ No ☐

5. Do you assess such opportunities and initiatives periodically? Yes ☐ No ☐

CHAPTER 11

THE NOISE

A few years ago, when my team and I were mandated to reform the sports sector in the Kingdom of Bahrain by one of our patrons, we set out an incredibly ambitious plan revolving around separating the sports sector from the youth affairs sector, then segregating the professional competitive sports sector from community sports and the "sports as a lifestyle" sector.

The project entailed that we create a new sports regulator entity, split the roles of operators from the roles of regulators, and further incorporate surgical changes to the incentivization system. We were also attempting to put in place mechanisms to ensure the independence of the executives working in the sector.

We had a full, four-year transformation program ahead of us that I fondly referred to as "Project 208," namely the number of weeks we had to achieve what in the beginning was deemed by many, including our own team, to be if not impossible, at least unfathomable.

But we had an excellent plan, and we got lucky. The resistance to change subsided much faster than we had anticipated once people started to see the impact and the effects of the new incentives taking root much sooner than I had anticipated. Slowly, meritocracy started to take root.

As far as the Project 208 project plan was concerned, by the first year, we were running at at least twice the speed that we had planned for. I had the usual weekly project status meetings with our patron every Monday, where I would continuously report that we were not only progressing—we were flying.

The fruits of our labor were being picked and harvested monthly, at times even weekly. We had local, regional, and, at times, international achievements to show for it. Not bad for a project management team that had absolutely no experience in sports except for arranging and executing corporate transactions pertaining to sports and sport infrastructure, but a team that nonetheless embodied and lived the Modern Alchemy method.

That said, after fourteen to eighteen months on the project and with buckets of achievements to prove our abilities for the informed to see, I arranged for a special session to assess the perception of our project patron, His Highness Sh. Nasser bin Hamad, with respect to how we were doing. I had a long questionnaire that I wanted to go through with him, which was distilled into one real question: "Of all of the things that can be done better (and there are always things that can be improved), what is the one thing that you would want us to focus on to fix?"

His answer stunned me and stunned the team. He gave me a one-word response. He said, "Noise."

You see, for the informed—the ones that are with us in the meetings, the ones that were seeing what we submitted behind closed doors, the ones reading the reports and seeing the institutional changes being made—we were running at breakneck speed, which led a number of times to be being told off by more senior colleagues in government with requests that we slow down. So, for the informed, we were indeed flying.

That said, His Highness's point was that for those outside the closed circuit—for the interested stakeholders outside our immediate circle; for the target audience, who had no way of deciphering what was causing these changes—there was absolutely no way for them to link the changes they could feel with changes being made deep within the machine and with the embedded algorithms.

Of course, His Highness was right. We had focused on the substance and forgot to prioritize the audience.

One takes it for granted that people will see the causal link between you being quietly hard at work and the fruits the institution is bearing. That is wrong; very few will make that link.

Needless to say, this was an easy fix institutionally. I assured our patron that we would incorporate Modern Alchemy's "inform and perform" into our project plan. And clearly, the inform element would take priority, as this was where we were coming short. We started focusing on noise.

Inform and Perform

How many incredible products can you think of that performed beautifully but did not survive over the long term, primarily because they did not communicate their value? How many brilliant scientists and engineers had their finds and their work buried in the archives of history only because they did not shed light on it enough? How many brilliant firms died only because they lacked rainmakers who could communicate their strengths to the right audience? How many countries lost out on international traffic and international opportunities because no one knew of their beauty or the strength of their offering?

It is clear, at times, that silence is deafening and, at other times, even deadly.

Declare It and Then Accomplish

The Arabs have a great bit of advice distilled in the saying, "Declared (i.e., said) and accomplished." This is what most people and organizations aspire to.

The purpose is clear for all to see. Declaring, then accomplishing, then repeating allows one to build momentum, build credibility, and gather a following.

If one goes back to the chapter called "The Opportunities," one considers that the main three values that we assess are resistance, resources required, and impact. A quick assessment of opportunities would validate that resistance is usually a significant barrier to capitalizing on any opportunity.

Constant and Consistent Noise Melts Resistance

Simply put, excessive amounts of noise (reinforced with validation through performance) targeted and delivered correctly over time simply melt away the resistance, allowing Alchemists to capitalize on more opportunities.

As was made clear, the opportunities tracker, the low-hanging fruits map, is not static and is continuously revisited, as the level of resistance and the resources required change over time, considering circumstances.

What one finds is that the targeted noise and constant shedding of light on partial achievement and performance allows one to melt away the resistance slowly to all supporters at an increasing pace. This only becomes greater if the narrative is refined so that one sees the logic of the messaging.

Example of Narrative Building

When we were developing the narrative for our Youth Sector Reform and Activation Program that we developed and executed for the Kingdom of Bahrain, we started with an overarching theme: the identity of the Bahraini youth.

We started by setting out our premise and our wholeheartedly stated belief that our Bahraini youth are identifiable and have a recognizable shared identity that transcends color, religion, creed, and so forth. Bahraini youth are special. They are recognizable by their value system—their love of competition, their aspiration for achievement, their ability to plan and execute long term, their collaborative nature, and their appreciation that delayed gratification pays dividends.

The number of Bahraini youth amounts to approximately four hundred thousand individuals out of a current global population of eight billion individuals. That makes them one in twenty thousand, signifying the rarity of these individuals.

The media messaging was initiated by reinforcing our pride in our Bahraini youth, consistently stating that "betting on our Bahraini youth is a sure bet." It continued by identifying our constituency as "precious"; they are the kingdom's most important resources and treasure, and their "mettle [i.e., what they're made of) is gold."

All the other programs we created fit within the parameters set out by these statements: that our Bahraini youths are "golden;" they "shine;" they can be challenged by circumstances and prevail; that they come together; that they're incorruptible;

that although they constitute only half of the present (i.e., half of the current population), they constitute all of the future.

For anyone hearing these aspirational statements, the message is clear. The message is that the kingdom's leadership is committed to investing in its youth.

Who Is Your Target Audience?

That said, when managing the noise, it is imperative that you know who your target audience is, a reality that is oddly lost in many initiatives and projects. Many times, we see amazing initiatives and projects that are launched and communicated in such a manner through a medium that simply cannot reach the target audience.

When picking the medium, when picking the message, one needs to start and end with the audience.

The simplest example that reflects such an occasion is the fault of using traditional printed media to reach a young target audience. Another nice example I was told once (I have not taken the time to verify this piece of folklore) is that Lamborghini does not advertise its products through television advertisements, arguing that its target audience is not made of couch potatoes.

Think of all the examples that you have come across where an advertiser or communicator got it all wrong, where they got the messenger, the message, and the medium wrong. It is always worth considering the logos, pathos, and ethos, which can be researched and addressed as part of the process.

For that reason, one starts and ends with the audience. Who are they? Where are they? How does one communicate with them?

Brilliant Examples of Targeted and Consistent Noise by States

There are a number of examples that simply set the bar in minimizing resistance and delivering messages through a targeted focus on noise delivery to a particular audience.

The first amongst many is the USA's brand. The United States of America has long recognized the importance of noise and has used it to its advantage exquisitely over time. One need only consider the messaging pertaining to projecting the military might and technological superiority of the United States for a fantastic benchmark.

The United States used the movies (i.e., Hollywood and others) medium brilliantly during the Cold War and thereafter, giving the audience (other military powers and counterparts) the perception that its capabilities were generations ahead of everyone else. There is no question that the message was well crafted and brilliantly delivered both directly and passively.

On the other hand, consider brand Dubai's brand—the world's safest destination, the playground of the rich and wealthy, and the new "land of opportunity." The perfectly manicured narrative projected around the world through product placement, through guerilla marketing of the highest quality, undoubtedly got the attention of the world's rich and famous—and those able to aspire to wealth and fame.

One would argue that billionaires and political leaders the world over today recognize Dubai as one of a handful of places where their security and the security of their assets can be guaranteed. This is reinforced by the exquisite execution of amazingly daring and incredibly public police operations periodically which show off the muscles of Dubai's security apparatus. Needless to say, petty criminals or even organized crime seem to opt for other jurisdictions after having digested Dubai's messaging.

Take a look also at Israel's secretive Mossad. They have now positioned themselves as an adversary that knows no territorial or bureaucratic legal limitations and is working to run operations (and, at times, executions) without any hesitation when it comes to crossing international borders. True or not, one would argue that the truth is irrelevant when an organization's target is seeing the idea and reinforcing the perception.

Think of Silicon Valley and how it has projected itself as the global hub of technology and creativity, which ends up being a self-fulfilling prophecy of its own. Talents believe the messaging, capital believes the narratives, and they both (talents and capital) meet in Silicon Valley.

Think of how Switzerland positioned itself as the world's banking capital, how London positioned itself as the global commerce capital, how Paris positioned itself as the capital of refinement, and how Japan positioned itself as the capital of craftsmanship. Think of all these and more, and one recognizes the importance of noise—of targeted, well-crafted, and consistently delivered noise.

Make It Loud, Make It Proud

It doesn't matter how amazing your work is if no one knows it exists, and results do *not* speak for themselves. You have to speak for them, and you have to convince everyone that these results are important. Rallying for support is a crucial part of the Alchemist's responsibility.

Now, this is not to downplay the necessity of action and performance, because in the end, performance and metrics matter.

Everyone wants to see what you've done and that you've done what you said you were going to do.

However, your journey Due North is a lot easier when you journey alongside allies, and as you make further progress, you will need more of them. To attract those allies to your cause, you must make noise—and not just a little bit of noise.

By getting the word out, you call attention to the cause and to your accomplishments to date, which lets you present and explain the results you've achieved. It's like building testimonials about your work, your direction, and your values.

If done correctly, communication builds credibility and puts one en route to building a cohesive, trusting environment.

Example – All Blacks Noise

For a sports example, we can look at the All Blacks, one of New Zealand's strongest rugby teams. Since 1903, they have won about 77 percent of the games they have been in; that alone speaks to their effectiveness across multiple personnel changes. Being part of a team with such a win record inspires confidence in the players and wows the prospects, but the All Blacks do not rely on this alone. Before every game, they do a dance called the *haka*. This dance serves to intimidate the opposing team, showing them that they are facing people who will not only crush them but also do it with a smile. The All Blacks will perform well not only because of their training but also because they are in a team that has to live up to its reputation.

One could say that faith plus hope equals confidence and that confidence is contagious. People notice when a person or organization is confident; it makes the organization look more professional and reliable. This confidence also has the effect of keeping competitors on their toes, since they aren't certain why your organization is so sure of itself.

This force of confidence is more powerful than you know.

Winning the War of Words

At times and in certain circumstances, wars of words are great for fostering noise. The war of words, the "us and them" element, at times reinforces cohesion between the team and rallies the proverbial troops.

When done well, your audience, your talents, your clients, and your customers don't just feel like they're paying for a product or a service; they're taking a value-based stance.

One need only consider the examples of Steve Jobs and Apple versus Bill Gates and Windows, of Richard Branson and Virgin Atlantic versus British Airways, of President Trump and President Biden. Further, many of the greats have a clear antagonist, from Puma and Adidas to Coca-Cola and Pepsi, and many, many more. All have clear counterparts that help define their own identity and help push them forward through competition.

The reality, whether we like it or not, is that we are judged by the company we keep, and we are judged by the brands, the projects, and the causes we support or follow. A true Alchemist can communicate well enough to bring into the fold like-minded, die-hard supporters, which can act as the core and whose corrective noise will resonate outwardly, creating the intended outcome.

Audit Your Noise

1. Does your organization focus on informing its stakeholders as much as it performs (or more)? Yes ☐ No ☐

2. Has your organization clearly declared its intentions? Yes ☐ No ☐

3. Have you prepared a narrative that can communicate your goals and direction in a seamlessly connected manner? Yes ☐ No ☐

4. Do you know who your target audience is? Yes ☐ No ☐

5. Have you decided how loud you need your noise to be? Yes ☐ No ☐

6. Do you have a counterpart that can assist in defining who you are and who you are not? Yes ☐ No ☐

CHAPTER 12

THE ENVIRONMENT

The purpose of this chapter is to attempt to demystify for aspiring Alchemists a key element that will support and reinforce the direction and trajectory of any organization: the environment.

We understand that aspiring Alchemists hear a lot about legacy tools, such as mission, vision, values, culture, and strategy, that have been adopted by consultants. The sad reality is that the interpretation of such terms and the use of such terms differs from one individual to another, thereby minimizing the value and benefit of the tools.

In this day and age, open almost any business plan or any website and you will see the headers "Mission," "Vision," and "Values" somewhere on the screen or in the business plan. The use of such terminology lacks consistency, having seeped into the business norms in different ways.

Worse yet, in other scenarios, one keeps hearing alternate soundbites that sound wise such as, "Culture eats strategy for breakfast," a phrase linked to Mr. Peter Drucker. That said, regurgitating such phrases without truly understanding the context or the terminology really doesn't help anyone—practitioners or the audience.

Alchemists would suggest an alternate, simpler view that attempts to make the tools and the benefits much clearer and concise and that provides guidance and clarity to the recipient. What we refer to as a "focus on environment" is one such tool.

What Is the Environment?

Simply put, the environment is the confined jurisdiction that is under the complete control of a group and is within the operating parameters of the organization. Therefore, for all intents and purposes, the environment is the sum of the area within the virtual boundaries of the organization.

And within this defined space, there must be an algorithmic and clear operating system that clearly sets out what may be expected from interactions internally. At times, it even gives insights into what can be expected when the organization interacts with others externally.

Within this proverbial jurisdiction, the algorithmic rules that are set out by the Alchemist are referred to as "values."

What Are Values?

There is a very interesting quote that Alchemists need to consider at this point which says, "You get what you accept." This applies to both individuals and organizations and, at times, to communities and countries. Therefore, clearly expressing what you do not accept is essential.

As mentioned, in the old traditional consulting lexicon, one keeps hearing from consultants about "missions, visions, and values," but the use of such terminology and its meaning changes from company to company, from consultant to consultant, and from media agency to media agency. The whole communicative aspect of the terms becomes somewhat redundant because everyone allocates differing meanings to the terms.

In the Alchemists' lexicon, the word "values" simply stands for everything that "you will not accept." Remember the quote, "You get what you accept." If true, the inverse is that you will not get what you do not accept.

Therefore, setting out clear and concise statements that clearly establish red lines that separate you from all the things you do not want within the limits of the organization's jurisdictional parameters is an extremely beneficial and productive exercise and provides immense clarity.

These statements and red lines can encompass anything that you will not accept during your journey toward your Due North. In other words, this will encompass, for example, the acts you will not condone, the patrons you will not serve, and the projects you will not accept.

Example of Values

Let me give you a relevant example of values. Let's say that you have a cycling team and their Due North is "faster." By definition, if they continue to follow their Due North, they will eventually be the fastest and, by virtue of that reality, will be number one on the podium.

That said, and as history has shown, there are many things that are unethical, immoral, and illegal that the team can do to become faster—everything from drugs to blood transfusions, from alteration of the equipment to sabotaging competing teams' equipment, and so on; the list is infinite.

Different teams and different communities have different red lines. What is reasonable in the eyes of one group may be completely unacceptable in the eyes of another.

And so, the values of a team or organization are the red lines that you will not cross. What will you simply not do or allow to be done even if it brings you closer to your Due North?

In the cycling domain example, one would have different teams and organizations that share different values and therefore different red lines. You would have the likes of the US Postal Service Discovery Channel Pro Cycling Team being led by Lance Armstrong, whose reports seem to run a clear "Don't get caught" value or red line with no limits on whether or not one should dope. On the other hand, the same team also had a clear "Do not report" value or red line which allowed its actions to continue for so long until Floyd Landis (a disgruntled, disqualified former team member) decided to initiate his legal federal whistleblower case which awarded him $1.1 million for whistleblowing.

One can transpose for comparison purposes the US Postal Service Discovery Channel Pro Cycling Team with Team Sky's stated values, which publicly adopted a clear "zero tolerance" policy for doping of any kind. As one can imagine, such a clear, solid red line marked in stone was also a challenge to honor, considering the fact that senior mature athletes were being recruited from other teams, who may have been more used to a less rigid approach. This in turn led to some interesting situations where Team Sky had to take action against players who had taken oral medication including triamcinolone, which the players claimed they took to treat severe allergies and asthma as opposed to performance enhancement.

Regardless of the outcomes of the two examples, the point is to establish that these are two very different sets of values adopted by two very different teams. The one element that both differing teams have is that people within the environment were very clear on the values of the team and the limits that were set.

Culture as a Result of Values

We hear a lot these days about culture. It's popular to discuss culture and to emphasize it in all organizations. I'd suggest that a good way to look at culture is the shared values in our definition of the word. Therefore, culture may be seen as a group's shared red lines.

Culture is simply what is revealed as a result of parameters drawn by shared values. Culture is therefore not a synthesized positive identity; it is actually the sum of clear statements on what this group is not.

As the reader would intuitively know, knowing what a thing is not draws the parameters of what the thing is and, at times, is as important as the positive statements.

A good way to understand this is to consider culture simply the sum of the shared values.

Key Values

The key to remember always is that an Alchemist has limited tools that they can rely on because of the inherent limitations of not being able or allowed by design to "touch the ball." The inability to be actively involved in the execution and the executive elements of the organization requires that Alchemists find another solution. It is for this reason that creating the right environment is so important by adopting clear values.

Here are a number of key values that are tried and tested and are recommended as a starting point.

Do Not Whisper

Generally speaking, and as a rule of thumb, "If you need to whisper it, don't say it."

Any organization thrives on goodwill and good communication. If someone has something to hide, it should stay hidden. People whisper when they're doing something wrong or when they're not sure how the team would react to something.

Jensen Huang of the now-famous Nvidia has a very interesting approach that embodies this value. It is said that in Nvidia, the CEO refuses to hold one-on-one meetings with his managers within the organization. The reasoning behind this is to ensure that there is no miscommunication within the organization and to equalize the amount of information that managers have; to confirm to all that nothing sinister is happening within the organization, which helps build faith; to minimize whisper campaigns and internal politicking within the organization; and to minimize the risk of micromanagement.

It must be said that Nvidia has grown tremendously. One wonders if this has a lot to do with it.

The logic behind the approach is quite simple. Whispering not only reveals a speaker's lack of faith in the task at hand, in the plan, in the parameters, and in the vision, but also leads others to do the same, breaking down hard-won trust and creating silos of information.

In addition, one risks turning the team members against each other and the leadership because of what you said, how it is interpreted, how it is executed, and the surprising nature of the outcome from the recipient colleague's perspective. It leads everyone to ask what else the speaker is hiding.

Whispering has another harmful effect—it harms the reputation of the firm even to outsiders. Should someone fall victim to a whisper campaign, your firm will gain a reputation as a shady or dangerous place, which hurts the organization's ability to recruit and retain talent.

Just as whisper campaigns can bring out what should stay hidden, they can also be used to keep things hidden that should come out. It is whisper campaigns that tend to keep victims of abuse or harassment from speaking out.

Transparency, stating problems out loud and assessing them analytically, allows everyone a chance to resolve issues and keeps things moving. Your competition and the challenges of life will not wait for you to get your organization in order. You must be ready at all times, and a culture of honesty, focused on solutions, can help you win.

Do Not Compensate Based on Effort or Time

One must always remember that the formula one uses to compensate talents signals to talents what one wants from them. When you understand this, it becomes clear that many organizations are miscommunicating their wants when one considers their compensation policy.

One very typical and recurring mistake that organizations make is to compensate people based on the time they have provided the organization without linking such remuneration to any other metric whatsoever. A simple example of such a situation is when companies agree to pay a recurring salary monthly, and at times pay for overtime, without a link to performance.

Few appreciate that by doing so, organizations are merely signaling that they want talents to allocate additional time to the organizations.

Therefore, what one finds when assessing such organizations is that people allocate an excessive amount of hours and naturally tend to prolong matters unnecessarily to gain recognition.

Another similar and equally (if not more) destructive mistake that organizations make is to link compensation to effort or, worse yet, compensate talents for flagging problems.

The reality of the matter is that individuals, particularly smart individuals, will always look for their benefit and will always try to "game" or figure out the best manner in which to maximize their individual returns. Therefore, incentivizing people based on their effort or their problem-finding efforts will only lead to the production of what we humorously refer to as "drama."

Think about it for a second. If the organization only responds to noise, talents will give you noise. If the organization only responds to performance, talents will give you performance.

What is key is the clarity with which what is wanted is communicated to the talents, through the adopted incentive structure. Therefore, when you compensate talents, do so based on their performance, not whatever notion you have about them, how they present themselves, what noise they create, and so forth.

Real talented people have no time to waste with internal political games, with inconsistency, or with unreliability. They will most definitely leave if they believe their skills aren't valued—and if they are not compensated in a manner that is linked to the value they bring. If one wants to retain real talents, aligning remuneration to the outcome needed is a good first step.

Example of How It Goes Wrong – The Cobra Effect

We are adamant that one must link the intended outcome of the talent's work with the remuneration to ensure alignment of interest. That said, history tells us that this can go wrong when not done correctly—and sometimes, the outcome is quite humorous though sad.

For example, let's take a look at the anecdotal events that transpired in India during the reign of the British Empire. The bureaucrats were concerned about the number of venomous snakes in the region and therefore simply adopted a program where each time an individual found and killed a venomous snake and handed it in, the act would translate into a good financial reward.

Needless to say, it didn't take long for people to hack the system and figure out that it took much less effort to breed the cobras in their houses and simply hand them in periodically to collect the rewards.

Sadly, as soon as the bureaucracy found out about the home-based "cobra farms," they discontinued the program, which led people to release the now-useless, venomous snakes. The outcome was a huge spike in the number of venomous snakes in the wild due to the introduction of the released population.

There are endless examples like this one, from the Great Hanoi Rat Massacre of 1902 to feral pig tail rewards adopted by the US Army in 2007 and many, many more from around the world. All backfired in the end.

Tenure versus Value – The Infamous Musk Example

The media had a field day when Elon Musk's long-time assistant decided to separate from his organizations. If one is to believe the media sources, it is claimed that Elon Musk once had an assistant who had been "loyally serving and supporting" him for twelve years during the period when he rose to serious global prominence. Notice the emphasis on loyalty, service, and support when the matter is being presented by the media while there is no reference to employment, contract, covenants, and engagement.

Because of the amount of time she had been working for him and the newfound success the companies had reached, she asked for a raise. She believed that the companies now had enough money and had to hand some of it over to her as an entitlement due to her tenure.

When the claim was made, there was, of course, no reference to the risk, if any, that she accepted during her employment, but it readily compared the amount she had made to date with those of investors who risked their capital. Needless to say, the request was assessed and the remuneration of her work was deemed to be in line with or possibly above market rates.

What's more, Musk opted to request that the assistant take an extended leave to better assess the responsibilities she was shouldering, the added value she provided, and how instrumental she was to the organization. They wanted to assess whether, as the assistant had suggested, her contribution to the running of the organization was crucial and foundational, therefore justifying significant remuneration. During the leave, it was found that her responsibilities could be simply redistributed to other staff members without any real interruption.

When confronted with this reality and the overall rejection of the request for pay, the media attacks commenced, focusing on the "tragedy" of unreciprocated loyalty and how she was "let go" after years of "service and support."

The point of the story is that the employer opted to stick to their values of not paying primarily based on tenure but instead to pay based on the value provided and created.

That said, the noise and the vengeful public attack with which this logical decision was met seem to show either a sense of entitlement or, worse yet, a miscommunication of values and expectations from the beginning. It almost seems as if she may have agreed to lower remuneration in the hope of sharing in the success of the company at a later date—which did not materialize when said success arrived.

We, of course, do not know the real details, but the lesson is clear: Communicate, communicate, communicate your values clearly.

Clarity not only results in higher profits and a calmer work culture; it also makes the organization more resistant to shocks and surprises, which in turn attracts phenomenal talents.

Do Not Corrupt the Decision-Making Process

When one creates a truly just environment, the outcome and the product are almost magical. When nothing matters except for the talents and their performance, and when everything is earned and can be explained simply, what eventually blossoms out of such a system is incredible. When decision-making, selection, and delegation are objective and when no animosity whatsoever exists, the level of cooperation and collaboration becomes phenomenal.

When any decision needs to be made, any stakeholder must be able to transparently see and understand why the decision was made, the logic behind it, and the impact of such a decision on the organization.

A meritocratic system is objective; either you get the results or you don't.

Let's look at the world of sports and the success of the community. Every federation or association invests endless amounts and hours to clarify the rules and, more importantly, to project a level playing field for all talents. Consider each sport to be a platform for talents, and consider the success that these platforms have reached.

Now, consider what happens to participation, to viewership, and to the overall sport when one finds examples where the "table was tilted in favor of one team versus the other." All it really takes is one clear example, just one breach, and the excitement, interest, and goodwill are lost—at times, forever.

Remember what happened to global cycling with the doping cases? Look at what happens in collegiate sports when match-fixing occurs and how long it takes to regain the trust of the public.

Now, superimpose that sports league example with democratic politics. Democratic politics provides an excellent measure when one considers the percentage of the respective voting populous that opts to vote. That number can tell you a lot about how the population feels about the matter.

Two lovely Arabic quotes come to mind when one considers that reality. The first says "Justice is the key foundation of governance." It is such a simple and intuitive statement, but sadly, few recognize the importance of such a "rule of law" approach and its impact on the overall environment.

The second says, "Either emirate [or kingship] or trade [or participation]." This simply means that a decision-maker cannot have a vested interest in the outcome. Again, it is intuitive to say the least and all should know it, but how many examples have you seen where the decision-maker that one adjudicates matters to has an interest in the outcome? How many times have you seen a member of a regulatory or supervisory body trade or compete in what he is regulating? Such situations kill the buy-in from the populous almost instantaneously and most definitely end all voluntary interactions eventually. This applies in all sectors.

Only when one considers that reality and considers the importance of the projection of the rule of law does one understand the importance of removing unjust practices if one is to continue to retain an audience and benefit from the buy-in. The simplest example is how people who enjoy watching or playing sports see the sporting federations as fair and therefore continue to interact.

It helps that sport is about transparency in action, so the physical nature of sports contributes to its perception of being just. Either you scored more points or you didn't; either you got first place or you didn't. Rarely does it get more complicated than that, although talks of corrupt umpires never end. Regardless, there's no argument, no way to politick your way to victory. Play better or perish.

This perception of meritocracy gives professional sports credibility in most people's eyes. Seeing how many sports fans exist, this is powerful because it shows that meritocracy has worldwide appeal.

Everyone wants to reward the job done well. Even when cheating happens, it doesn't harm belief in the meritocratic ideal—as long as the effort to weed out such activities is real and can readily be seen by all.

Just the same, your organization should be a meritocracy because not only will top talent show up and stay, but it will also make the organization's leadership just in the eyes of people at large—and that is where the real magic happens.

Do Not Allow Bad Leavers Into Your Organization

Organizations work with their talents to create values and systems and build institutions and goodwill over time.

Yet many times, the very same talents destroy all that was co-created, whether it is the teams, the reputation, or the systems, on their way out. Those are what we refer to as "bad leavers." The amount of destruction that they cause far exceeds any value they create during their tenure.

The most important element, one would argue, when recruiting is to look first at their employment and partnership history. When assessing whether to allow talents into the organization or not, it's essential to assess the relationship talents have with their previous employers and, more importantly, whether they are earmarked as "bad leavers," meaning destructive leavers.

If they have left an organization and breached covenants, such as theft of IP, solicitation of clients and personnel, attacking the previous employer's reputation, and so forth, then such an individual should not be allowed into your organization because nature dictates that they will probably do the same with you.

If it is inevitable that one will interact with them due to certain skill sets, then one can always have them as a Contractor or vendor delivering products or services at arm's length—but nothing more.

Do Not Tip the Scale of Justice

Think about all the organizations and, for that matter, the countries that come to mind. Now, think of the successful ones over time. They all have one thing in common. When the rules are clear, when justice is transparent and consistent, amazing outcomes start to appear. Talents and capital will flock away from injustice and chaos and toward justice and security and, in so doing, will create amazing things, if allowed the freedom to collaborate and cooperate.

Having great or even absolute power and therefore absolute discretion on its own isn't enough to allow an organization to flourish. In those instances, one can micromanage all they want (and on rare occasions, even find examples of nano-management)—it will not help anything and will only suffocate the organization. Everything will move at the pace of the weakest link (i.e., the micro/nano-manager). Simply put, it won't work.

Instead, clear parameters, clear circumstances, and consistency of outcomes can turn even a desert rock into a lush, heavenly garden over time. But remember that one doesn't get too many chances to protect the sanctity of the place (i.e., the scales of justice). All it takes is a few bad examples of interference and preferential treatment, and the cause is lost for at least a generation.

History has endless examples scattered throughout it, from Lee Kuan Yew's rule of law approach to King Leopold's discretionary absolutist approach and many, many others on the spectrum.

One thing is clear: Clarity and consistency create grounds for an environment of objectivity and meritocracy because they make clear what behavior is expected and what behavior is forbidden. They also reinforce your organization's mission and direction.

By contrast, ruling by arbitrary whim puts everyone on edge because they have no idea what behavior will get them thrown out. The mission changes from week to week, making it hard to establish a core set of values.

The arbitrary, discretionary approach does not work in the long term. No one would work hard for future gain if the future were not predictable and the reward were not clear and guaranteed. Without any consistency, there'd be nothing to aim for.

Do Not Show Favoritism or Support Nepotism

If you're going to attract the best, statistically the best are probably not your siblings; they are probably not your family members; they are probably not from your extended family; and they probably are not even from your friends and acquaintances network. They are probably individuals who have been brought up very far from where you reside. They probably grew up in very different circumstances and they probably are not within your immediate network.

One thing is for sure: If you show any sign of nepotism or unearned or unexplainable, and therefore unachievable, favoritism, then you will lose their buy-in much sooner than you think.

They are not part of your family and can never change their background to become a biological descendant of your ancestors. Therefore, that is a route simply lost.

All talents look to be favored and, by extension, trusted and remunerated. If they cannot simply see the route to such a favored pedestal, if the path is not crystal clear because they needed to be born in your family, the talents will eventually opt to invest their time and energy elsewhere.

Do Not Judge Talents by Their Looks

Never assume that talents of a particular function physically look a particular way, have a particular color, or are from a particular place. For example, do not assume that all honest accountants project an image of religious devotion. Some of the most unethical acts historically have been done by individuals who project the most pious of images.

The key here is to judge talents based on their actions and their history of delivering value and shouldering responsibility, not on the image that they attempt actively to project.

One of the simplest summaries of the lesson of focusing on actions and not words or images is found in the Bible, in Matthew 7:15–20:

> *"Beware of false prophets, who come to you in sheep's clothing, but inwardly they are ravenous wolves. You will know them by their fruits. Do men gather grapes from thornbushes or figs from thistles? Even so, every good tree bears good fruit, but a bad tree bears bad fruit. A good tree cannot bear bad fruit, nor can a bad tree bear good fruit. Every tree that does not bear good fruit is cut down and thrown into the fire. Therefore, **by their fruits, you will know them**."*

Therefore, always remember to focus on their "fruits" (i.e., actions and deliverables). And when the assessment of their "fruits" leads you to a conclusion, good or bad, do not ignore the analytics just because of their outward appearance.

A good quote to remember is, "When people show you who they are [through their actions and omissions], believe them."

Do Not Search for Talents in a Closed Pool
When recruiting talents, keep the proverbial "net" cast as open as possible, because you don't know where the gems might come from.

The assumption that gems come from a particular place is not always right. That assumption will not serve you well and will force you to compete with the very same talents that everyone else is competing for, thereby forcing you to expend unnecessary resources.

Malcolm Gladwell, in his book called *The Myths of Meritocracy: A Revisionist History Anthology*, goes on to present his findings that assuming good talents come out of certain institutions or locations is simply wrong. For example, he shows that although some recruiters and employers will only recruit from academic institutions like Harvard, the reality of the matter is that when analyzed, which academic institution one graduates from has no correlation whatsoever with how well a candidate does in the job.

This, of course, is shocking, considering the legacy assumption that the "great" universities produce great recruits. This is particularly shocking for individuals who spent fortunes purchasing an association with such a level of prestige.

That said, this finding simply means that there are stellar pools of unknown and undervalued talents that the majority are not tapping into who are ripe and ready to be picked, with minimal competition from recruiters.

This reality means that every organization has an opportunity to compete for talent as long as they keep the "net" as open as possible.

Don't Surprise Anyone

Simply put, real talents do not like surprises.

Talents require a place that embodies the following traits to flourish: **predictability**, **openness**, **competition**, and **justice**.

It's that simple, in theory. There is more to it in practice, so that's what we'll cover next.

But at every interval and what is key, one must be **predictable**. This allows talents to try to calmly figure out how to harmonize and work with you and others. The sooner harmonization is reached, the sooner the "magic" happens.

But on *your* end, from an organization's perspective, it's best when your words match your actions, because then it means that you will do what you say you will do every time.

Being just is not about being the nicest, being the most casual, or putting on the best appearance. It is about being predictable and consistent. When a new person comes in, they will not only know the written rules, but the unwritten ones as well because they will align with the written rules.

It is on this basis that your performance will be judged. To allow a just meritocracy to reign, you must lay out the parameters for measuring everyone's performance—do A, get B. It must be that clear so that no one will be nervous about where they stand.

If one person does all the work but you promote someone else, this destroys any perception of fairness or justice, so make sure the high performers are always rewarded in public to reinforce the idea.

Another thing you must do is make the logic behind the decision-making process transparent. If certain decisions are made about the company, state the reasoning and logic whenever asked. Do not create any occasion for a whisper campaign to begin. If you don't do this, you risk looking arbitrary, making decisions based on personal whims. The same goes for choosing people to work on a project. They have to be the person best suited to the task; otherwise, it looks like you chose them due to favoritism rather than merit.

This approach has a positive social effect: It reduces jealousy and therefore speeds up harmonization. Because the only 'favorites' are those who perform, there's no feeling that someone was chosen due to personal preference.

The rules apply equally to everyone, and everyone's responsibilities are clear. No one will have extra work dumped on them, nor will they be given someone else's responsibilities while the original person coasts.

You can't have any hidden agendas, and you can't have hidden biases, either. Everything has to be crystal clear to everyone. Fewer jealous people mean fewer chances of being backstabbed or sabotaged—and if it does happen, that person can be isolated.

Deliverables have to be written down in black and white, clear to all. To minimize politics, these deliverables have to be based on objective, quantifiable criteria.

For the sake of transparency, the employee must know three things: what to deliver, when to deliver it, and what would happen when they do. This predictability will motivate people to get the job done because they know that every time they do, something good will happen.

Asking for these results has another benefit too: It forces you to be honest about your employees' skills. If the employees aren't getting what they want, you must tell them that it's because their skills aren't up to your standards and they have failed to reach the deliverables that you have asked for. There's no dancing around it, no generic fluff to give them about anything at all. You have to sit down with the employees and assess their performance. If they're lacking, they're just not good enough, and that's why they've fallen behind.

Remember, this evaluation has to be objective.

For example, Netflix forces the conversation and the confrontation. Every employee at the end of every year goes through an exercise to find out what their market value is. Then, they tell the managers what the market says. They say, "I believe my service to the organization is worth in the market X amount per year. Are you willing to match this?" After that, the employer and the employee have that conversation, ending with a yes or no decision, with clarity with regard to the logic.

Regardless of whether they agree on advancement or if the employee opts to be relieved of their duties, in all cases, the organization populous understands and believes that the conversation and the decisions revolve around logic and markets, not individual discretion. Therefore, there is no negative ripple effect that is felt within the organization.

Another good reason and a positive side effect to creating a predictable, open, competitive environment with clear goals is to sniff out toxic individuals with high, unearned levels of entitlement or unreasonably high levels of expectations. People like Musk's previous assistant come to mind, based on the published stories—people who believe they deserve more than what you're paying them right now in lieu of their service but who do not know the real market value of such service.

If everyone knows the score, no one can complain publicly (or, arguably, privately), but when it's not clear, people can get resentful and you have no clue it's happening. Such people become jealous, start whisper campaigns, and make the work environment toxic for everyone. Because these types of people and their sentiments remain hidden, they can cause issues for you that will blow up when you least expect them to.

Resentment seeps into everything those bad actors do. They'll deliver low-quality work not for lack of ability but because they see you as unworthy of respect. They will conspire against you because they believe they're righting a great wrong—and don't forget, most people see themselves as the hero. They'll obstruct you or their co-Associates, hoping to slow things down without being noticed.

All this happens because they want to avoid conversations about what they bring to the table. What are their skills? What good have they done? They won't be able to answer those questions, so they will stonewall as much as possible. Make sure such people are ferreted out and removed at once. Having everyone evaluated on performance will do that job in such a way that they cannot object using politics—they didn't do their job as specified, so they're out of luck.

Your organization will become known for quality and fairness, and only the best performers will progress to the top. You will do well, and it will seem like a miracle.

This is Modern Alchemy—you have become a miracle worker. You have turned what seemed like lead into pure gold. As long as you keep your mission in mind and cut out everything and everyone who doesn't align with that mission, you will go far and ascend to heights undreamed of, and your talent will thank you for it. Then the next generation of top talents will come.

Every general in any army knows that if you are predictable, talents will join and will march for you and the cause. If there is no predictability, if the spoils of war are sometimes distributed and sometimes aren't depending on individual whims, they will not march, and rightly so. Talents need to trust that the organization will honor their commitments in all circumstances.

Audit Your Environment

1. Has your organization built a transparent meritocracy that emphasizes a predictable, open, competitive, and just environment so that you're prepared to attract top talent? Yes ☐ No ☐

2. Are the rules of your organization clearly communicated, explained, and posted to all employees? Yes ☐ No ☐

3. Are all employees, no matter their rank, held equally accountable to your organization's rules (to ensure a level playing field)? Yes ☐ No ☐

4. Does each task in your organization have a black-and-white deliverable, destination for that deliverable, and expectation for what should occur once that deliverable reaches its destination? Yes ☐ No ☐

5. Is your management equipped to have honest, blunt conversations with your talent to establish expectations and highlight places for improvement? Yes ☐ No ☐

6. Does your organization allot time for employees to self-assess and then present their fair market value to ensure that employees feel justly compensated for their time and skills? Yes ☐ No ☐

CHAPTER 13

THE HOPE AND FAITH

When one studies Modern Alchemy, there is no question that all projects or organizations are limited in their achievement by the ability of the talents within the organization and the ability of those talents to focus on the direction while harmonizing, synchronizing, and complimenting their efforts with the drum.

Simply put, all great projects are the product of skilled group efforts. They all tend to be multi-generational in that they cannot be done from start to finish in one lifetime, and they all survive only if the momentum can be sustained.

Recently, I visited France. While I was at a museum participating in a guided tour, the guide noted several beautiful sculptures and how many years each one took to go from concept to completion. While admiring the lovely stonework, I realized something: Some of those figures consumed the majority of the sculptor's entire lifetime. And that lifetime, despite all the hard effort it took to make such works of art, was not even enough to fill a room. One person can only do so much.

Regardless of that fact, when one dissects the organization into its units, one will inevitably reach down to the individual member.

What Makes Individuals March?

This question is one that leads to a key understanding that is essential to any organization, regardless of its industry and the context of the mission. To understand Modern Alchemy, one needs to meditate on this question for a while to get a better understanding.

Think about it for a second. Go back in time. What makes an artilleryman on the front lines of a battlefield like Waterloo take his shot, then reload, then stand up straight to wait for the other side to shoot at him, only because it's their turn to shoot? What makes a person do that? To accept the risks associated with standing on the front lines waiting for bullets to fly in his direction, and to do so without any complaints?

Go back further. What makes a seafaring captain and his men attempt to cross unknown and unchartered seas to find new lands and riches? When the outcome is unknown and the path is unchartered, why would they risk so much?

Our answer in Modern Alchemy is simple: hope and faith.

What Do We Mean by Hope and Faith?

The question is, what makes men (and women) march? Better yet, what makes them march when the outcome is unknown? Experience and observations dictate that it's both hope and faith. This is what drives us all.

It is human nature, sadly, to be unsatisfied with the status quo. We all have something that triggers us, some source of nuisance, something that can be better. Therefore, we all have the current state and the future intended state in our minds all the times. And we all have the hope that sometime in the future, that better future intended state will be the new reality and the new norm.

Simply put, we all want to believe that tomorrow will be better than today with respect to those elements that are gnawing at us and annoying us.

Hope, as it is referred to in Modern Alchemy, is the energy one has to move forward on the basis that forward, or the future, will be better than the current state. It is the energy that gets one out of the sun and into the shade. It is the energy that gets one to walk up a mountain trail for better weather.

We have explained what hope is in the Modern Alchemy lexicon. Faith compliments hope. Where hope is the drive to move forward, faith is the knowledge or assumption that this route is the best route to get to the intended future state, free from the stated identified nuisance. Hope is the drive that pushes you forward, and faith is the knowledge and belief that this is the correct route.

In our corporate context, hope is their belief that the nuisance of not having sufficient funds can be alleviated if the right plan is executed. Faith is their belief that joining your organization and investing their time and energy with you is the right route or path to alleviate the nuisance.

Remember that even an employee who works for a basic monthly salary must have hope and faith. They have hope that they will get paid for their work, and they must have faith that the employer will not renege on their deal or that they will have the funding in place to make the payment in the future. One needs to remember that the service always precedes the reward, which means that every service provider, regardless of the form, must have faith that contracts and words will be honored.

It is only when these two elements meet that achievements become a real possibility.

The clearest sign that hope and faith exist within a talent pool or an individual talent is the presence of confidence in how they carry themselves while doing the work. The surest way to identify if hope and faith are lacking is to assess individual talents' micro-perceptions, or figuring out whether they feel safe, seen, supported, wanted, and trusted. This is an incredibly powerful tool to establish the health of the situation and the level of drive within the talent and the group.

In effect, what it is actually gauging is whether talents feel safe and if they feel respected. These are actually the two big pillars that people aspire to have but historically find it difficult to communicate.

History is littered with examples of organizations and projects that failed to pay attention to individual signs and perceptions, whether we're talking about the European colonial empires, the Tokugawa shogunate in Japan, or the old Soviet Union. Once the people collectively decide that a project or style of government cannot work or that an objective cannot be met, that organization or power dissolves because it cannot stay strong without the faith of the people to bolster and sustain it. To make matters worse, there are no second chances when this loss of faith occurs. Just as there will be no restoration of the Roman Empire, there will be no rise from the ashes for a company that collapses after its team loses faith in its direction. Lost confidence is hard, if not impossible, to regain. You're better off starting something new from square one, free from the baggage of the old ways, because everyone wants to be part of the new thing that's going into the future, not the old thing that is stuck looking back on days gone by.

This is why you must keep your talents confident with hope and faith.

Trajectory and Momentum versus Culture and Strategy

In chapter 1, I stated that what matters more to an organization's success than either culture or strategy is trajectory and momentum. This is not to say that neither culture nor strategy have their place; they do. Culture has appeared throughout this book, but it's always been in the context of an outcome, not a "to-do." Culture is not something you *do*; it's something you foster *as a result* of other actions.

We have focused this chapter on hope and faith. Nothing is more important in increasing hope and faith than loudly and proudly building and celebrating an upward trajectory and increased momentum.

The reality of the matter is that we humans have an innate fear of missing out. We have a fear that the tribe will march and leave us behind. We have a fear that others will develop and leave us behind. We have a fear that we will make the wrong decision and take the wrong turn or miss the opportunity when it comes knocking that one time.

It is clearly documented in scientific papers that loss and fear of loss are much higher drivers in people than any form of gain. So, the risk of losing is much worse for us than the chance of gaining.

It is for this reason that certain corporations have come up with the ingenious idea of, instead of giving talents opportunities to gain bonuses, talents are handed the bonuses or shares in advance, but said bonuses or shares are clawed back when targets are not met. Although the numerical values are exactly the same, the outcome and the drive are completely different.

Therefore, losing something that one has in their hand or losing an opportunity that one had to gain is far more potent than any potential future gain or reward due to performance. It is for this reason that nothing is more beneficial to growing hope and faith than building momentum and having an upward trajectory. Also true is that nothing is more destructive to hope and faith than losing momentum or trajectory.

Humanity's history is riddled with examples of proverbial corporate ships that have been abandoned because the momentum has slowed, where talents simply assumed an ultimate demise inevitable or, worse yet, that an opportunity to join a better, bigger, and faster ship is being lost. It is for this reason that one must manage the narrative pertaining to the increasing momentum and upward trajectory very carefully; it can truly make or break a turnaround project.

A key example of this was one readily shared by Jeff Bezos when he talked about the beginning of Amazon and how investors were shorting his stock although the numbers and earnings were decent, only for it to turn into pro-Amazon mania when momentum started to build. The herd of investors rushed to leave when there was a slowdown and rushed to buy back when the momentum was expressed and presented correctly. In both circumstances, their readings and their reactions were too exaggerated.

Continuous Storytelling

Faith isn't just about the job itself—it also involves the employees, and the best way to generate faith is by providing opportunities. It's not enough to say that when you work here for X years, you get Y benefits, or that people who do X get Y; you have to make it real for them.

Highlight success stories not only about projects but also about individuals, and make sure to highlight what role the individual played. To encourage the interns, tell stories about interns who did excellent work. To encourage the accountants, tell stories about clever and smart-working accountants. To encourage the customer service reps, tell stories about reps who made excellent decisions that led to great results, and so on and so forth.

Make sure to repeat this kind of thing. The modern environment is one where everyone is addicted to social media, and things pass out of the mind extremely quickly. The only way to have staying power is to stay in their minds, and that means repetition. So over and over, make it clear that advancement happens in your firm. Just like with the public and the media, employees have to receive this motivational message regularly and often.

But even this isn't enough; it takes more than a promise of promotion to make an organization work. Your rules must be consistent and clear; this way, everyone knows how to achieve success. If you change the rules all the time, or if you play favorites, you will poison the atmosphere. Merit, or how well someone gains results, must be the measure of all things, and this cannot be overstated.

To underline this point, let us take the biggest, most famous example: the United States of America. The country has an ideal of meritocracy—that those who do the best job should be the ones to lead. "Life, liberty, and the pursuit of happiness" are the ideals to strive for. This contrasts with the old idea, held in many world cultures, that birth and bloodlines determine one's station in life. The chance for even a poor man to make something of himself has attracted millions to America's shores. There's a good reason it's called the "Land of Opportunity."

A system of meritocracy shows a clear path to success—if you do X, you will not only receive Y but you will also be justified in doing so. This increases morale and thus faith in the organization, because the person knows that they got the result and the reward through their own efforts, not because someone just decided to hand it to them. It will give them hope.

Example – Getting Singapore to March in Unison

Singapore shouldn't have been able to become a first-world state but it did, all because of one consequential ruler: Lee Kuan Yew.

Before Lee's rise to power in 1959, Singapore was a poverty-stricken mess under British colonial rule. An invasion from Japan had done it no favors either. Stuck in an unfavorable position with no natural resources, Singapore should have turned out like so many postcolonial countries—basket cases full of corruption and political instability.

But this didn't happen to Singapore—instead, it became the picture of law, order, and good government. Because Lee took that long shot and had the faith and the hope that Singapore could rise, he moved heaven and earth to create systems of governance that promoted stability, even at the controversial expense of democracy or equality. He succeeded beyond his wildest dreams—the result was a first-world economy with a high standard of living that regional competitors could never hope to match.

The point of the Singapore example is to show how powerful the combination of faith and hope can be, even when going against Western ideals such as democratic freedom. Lee did not hire doubters and complainers for his civil service, and he had absolute confidence that the systems he put in place would survive his retirement—and they did.

One thing that Lee Kuan Yew was famous for was his reminders. He would remind the Singaporeans at every interval that nothing about the state's success is normal or natural. It was all unnatural, built on the harmonized discipline of their talents. The key lesson from Lee Kuan Yew is to remind the team constantly.

The Fragility of Hope and Faith

One should never underestimate the fragility of hope and faith. From them to be present, the predictability of the algorithm for success within the organization and the predictability and reliability of the leadership, each with their immediate line manager all the way up the organization ladder, must be sacrosanct. Under no circumstances should anything be done or said that may question the predictability or reliability of the organization's rules or its leadership's promise to enforce those rules.

For example, a low-ranking employee has faith that the leadership will track the performance of the employees and will financially compensate members based on their performance and not based on any other metric, including but not limited to nepotism, altruistic empathy, or duration of employment.

We've all heard and seen the impact of leadership giving a reward to an individual member of the workforce by way of empathetic charity but at the cost of the others and what such action does to overall morale within the organization. Handouts are, at times, as poisonous to the overall organization's cause and momentum as nepotism, corruption, or incompetence.

Therefore, one needs to beware. All actions are being observed and analyzed closely by the community, and there are no real secrets that can be kept hidden for long periods of time within any form of organization. It is therefore prudent and essential to walk the talk and ensure that the formula for success within the organization is crystal clear for all to see and test.

What's in a Few Words

Hope and faith switch on and off like light bulbs and tend to be quite binary. One action might switch on the hope and faith and the second might switch them off.

It is for this reason that one is always one or two wrong steps away from switching off a talent's hope and faith and must therefore tread very carefully and gently.

With regret, we have seen examples where a professional lifetime's worth of hope and faith is destroyed because of a few words said on behalf of the organization, making the whole positive illusion of camaraderie, alignment, and common cause pop like a bubble.

Anybody who has worked for long enough has seen leaders issue one statement in private stating, "All of you can be fired and replaced immediately and can be sent home if you continue your chatter," leading to an instantaneous disengagement by the key talents.

We have all seen unquestionable, romanticized, long-term loyalty and alignment popped by a single statement to customers and counterparts half-jokingly saying, "I hope he's treated you well [i.e., your relationship manager that we appointed]. If not, we'll remove him now and simply appoint another one [i.e., relationship manager]." One sentence said in jest destroys any remnants of hope and faith and starts the talent's journey of quiet migration, and rightly so.

If there is not a set formula or algorithm that dictates success within the organization, if it is based on the absolute whim and discretion of an individual with no inclination or clarity on what is good or not, what is accepted or not, what is wanted or not, hope and faith cannot be sustained for too long. One outburst can start a "bank run" for indemnities for outgoing talents.

Simply put: Be warned. Hope and faith are more fragile than most people think.

Attacks on Hope and Faith

We have already spoken about talents, how to categorize such talents, and how to weed them out, but one element needs to be stated clearly and repeated here unequivocally.

If any Partner, Contractor, or Associate publicly attacks hope and faith in any setting and in front of his subordinates, that individual must be removed immediately from the organization; the damage caused by the delay will far outweigh the damage caused by his removal, regardless of who that person is. If the person attacks that "tomorrow can and will be brighter [hope]," and if the person attacks that "this plan to march together can and will work [faith]," the person has to go. The higher the individual is in the organization, the faster he should leave. There is nothing more important than serenity and protection of hope and faith.

It is for this reason that we see wise organizations like Netflix and others periodically adopting a program whereby they would reward and pay those of low hope and faith for accepting to leave the enclave of the organization, an effort we applaud.

Beware of Those Who Are Satiated

We have presented the importance of momentum and trajectory in our journey, and we tried to describe the almost magical foundational role of hope and faith and the necessity to protect them as a high-priority item.

One of the risks to hope and faith comes from satiated, lethargic talents who are good at what they do, honorable, and aligned, but simply satiated or "full," regardless of how big or amazing the mission seems. The key tell of a satiated talent is that they have no intended future state. They have reached where they want to reach and are happy with their status quo and, by extension, the organization's status quo.

If that feeling is not shared by the organization, then such talent can be destructive to the hope and faith of the others around them and the organization as a whole.

Unified March

Selecting the name "Modern Alchemy" was purposely done to conjure time-old tales of mysticism, magic potions, and divine interventions. This was only done because when a Modern Alchemist succeeds in unifying a group of talents's pace and march in a particular direction in unison, with perfect alignment and harmonized movements, something magical seems to happen—something at par with the classics, the biblical stories, the timeless narrations that have stood the test of time.

I hope that you have an opportunity, if once, to feel the supernatural sensation of being more than just an individual when you truly become part of a whole, a body of people, with a unified march to a better tomorrow.

Audit Your Faith

1. Does your company have a clear model for rewarding based on merit alone to inspire employees to have faith in the leadership's integrity? Yes ☐ No ☐

2. Are your roles assigned to employees based on a good personality alignment rather than an alignment of skill sets (which can always be learned later, if needed)? Yes ☐ No ☐

3. Does your company have a regular plan to demonstrate confidence and a plan for organization-wide cooperation to bolster this confidence? Yes ☐ No ☐

4. Has your company communicated a cooperative view to its entire team of employees, letting them see that they each play a vital task in an effort that could not be accomplished without every single one of them? Yes ☐ No ☐

5. Have you categorized your employees into the categories of choir, converts, mercenaries, or containment to determine how to best care for and manage them? Yes ☐ No ☐